Poems of Nature, Poems Subjective and Reminiscent

Volume II., The Works of Whittier: by John Greenleaf Whittier

Table of Contents

Table of Contents

Table of Contents

Table of Contents

Table of Contents

Poems of Nature, Poems Subjective and Reminiscent

Volume II., The Works of Whittier: by John Greenleaf Whittier

Kessinger Publishing reprints thousands of hard−to−find books!

Visit us at http://www.kessinger.net

Poems of Nature, Poems Subjective and Reminiscent

- A MYSTERY.
- A SEA DREAM.
- HAZEL BLOSSOMS.
- SUNSET ON THE BEARCAMP.
- THE SEEKING OF THE WATERFALL.
- THE TRAILING ARBUTUS
- ST. MARTIN'S SUMMER.
- STORM ON LAKE ASQUAM.
- A SUMMER PILGRIMAGE.
- SWEET FERN.
- THE WOOD GIANT
- A DAY.

- POEMS SUBJECTIVE AND REMINISCENT MEMORIES

- RAPHAEL.
- EGO.
- THE PUMPKIN.
- FORGIVENESS.
- TO MY SISTER,
- MY THANKS,
- REMEMBRANCE
- MY NAMESAKE.
- A MEMORY
- MY DREAM.
- THE BAREFOOT BOY.
- THE WAITING.
- SNOW–BOUND.
- MY TRIUMPH.
- IN SCHOOL–DAYS.
- MY BIRTHDAY.
- RED RIDING–HOOD.
- RESPONSE.
- AT EVENTIDE.
- VOYAGE OF THE JETTIE.
- MY TRUST.

Poems of Nature, Poems Subjective and Reminiscent

- A NAME
- GREETING.
- AN AUTOGRAPH.
- ABRAM MORRISON.
- A LEGACY

- RELIGIOUS POEMS

  - THE CITIES OF THE PLAIN
  - THE CALL OF THE CHRISTIAN
  - THE CRUCIFIXION.
  - PALESTINE
  - HYMNS.
  - THE FAMILIST'S HYMN.
  - EZEKIEL
  - WHAT THE VOICE SAID
  - THE ANGEL OF PATIENCE.
  - THE WIFE OF MANOAH TO HER HUSBAND.
  - MY SOUL AND I
  - WORSHIP.
  - THE HOLY LAND
  - THE REWARD
  - THE WISH OF TO–DAY.
  - ALL'S WELL
  - INVOCATION
  - QUESTIONS OF LIFE
  - FIRST–DAY THOUGHTS.
  - TRUST.
  - TRINITAS.
  - THE SISTERS
  - "THE ROCK" IN EL GHOR.
  - THE OVER–HEART.
  - THE SHADOW AND THE LIGHT.
  - THE CRY OF A LOST SOUL.
  - ANDREW RYKMAN'S PRAYER
  - THE ANSWER.

- THE ETERNAL GOODNESS.
- THE COMMON QUESTION.
- OUR MASTER.
- THE MEETING.
- THE CLEAR VISION.
- DIVINE COMPASSION.
- THE PRAYER–SEEKER.
- THE BREWING OF SOMA.
- A WOMAN.
- THE PRAYER OF AGASSIZ.
- IN QUEST
- THE FRIEND'S BURIAL.
- A CHRISTMAS CARMEN.
- VESTA.
- CHILD–SONGS.
- THE HEALER.
- THE TWO ANGELS.
- OVERRULED.
- HYMN OF THE DUNKERS
- GIVING AND TAKING.
- THE VISION OF ECHARD.
- INSCRIPTIONS.
- ON A FOUNTAIN.
- BY THEIR WORKS.
- THE WORD.
- THE BOOK.
- REQUIREMENT.
- HELP.
- UTTERANCE.
- ORIENTAL MAXIMS.
- LAYING UP TREASURE
- CONDUCT
- AN EASTER FLOWER GIFT.
- THE MYSTIC'S CHRISTMAS.
- AT LAST.
- WHAT THE TRAVELLER SAID AT SUNSET.

POEMS OF NATURE

POEMS SUBJECTIVE AND REMINISCENT

RELIGIOUS POEMS

BY
JOHN GREENLEAF WHITTIER

POEMS OF NATURE

THE FROST SPIRIT

He comes,—he comes,—the Frost Spirit comes
    You may trace his footsteps now
On the naked woods and the blasted fields and the
    brown hill's withered brow.
He has smitten the leaves of the gray old trees
    where their pleasant green came forth,
And the winds, which follow wherever he goes,
    have shaken them down to earth.

He comes,—he comes,—the Frost Spirit comes!
    from the frozen Labrador,
From the icy bridge of the Northern seas, which
    the white bear wanders o'er,
Where the fisherman's sail is stiff with ice, and the
    luckless forms below
In the sunless cold of the lingering night into
    marble statues grow

He comes,—he comes,—the Frost Spirit comes
    on the rushing Northern blast,
And the dark Norwegian pines have bowed as his
    fearful breath went past.
With an unscorched wing he has hurried on,
    where the fires of Hecla glow
On the darkly beautiful sky above and the ancient
    ice below.

He comes,—he comes,—the Frost Spirit comes
    and the quiet lake shall feel

6

The torpid touch of his glazing breath, and ring to
    the skater's heel;
And the streams which danced on the broken
    rocks, or sang to the leaning grass,
Shall bow again to their winter chain, and in
    mournful silence pass.
He comes,—he comes,—the Frost Spirit comes!
    Let us meet him as we may,
And turn with the light of the parlor–fire his evil
    power away;
And gather closer the circle round, when that
    fire–light dances high,
And laugh at the shriek of the baffled Fiend as
    his sounding wing goes by!
1830.

THE MERRIMAC.

"The Indians speak of a beautiful river, far to the south,
which they call Merrimac."—SIEUR. DE MONTS, 1604.

Stream of my fathers! sweetly still
The sunset rays thy valley fill;
Poured slantwise down the long defile,
Wave, wood, and spire beneath them smile.
I see the winding Powow fold
The green hill in its belt of gold,
And following down its wavy line,
Its sparkling waters blend with thine.
There 's not a tree upon thy side,
Nor rock, which thy returning tide
As yet hath left abrupt and stark

Above thy evening water–mark;
No calm cove with its rocky hem,
No isle whose emerald swells begin
Thy broad, smooth current; not a sail
Bowed to the freshening ocean gale;
No small boat with its busy oars,
Nor gray wall sloping to thy shores;
Nor farm–house with its maple shade,
Or rigid poplar colonnade,
But lies distinct and full in sight,
Beneath this gush of sunset light.
Centuries ago, that harbor–bar,
Stretching its length of foam afar,
And Salisbury's beach of shining sand,
And yonder island's wave–smoothed strand,
Saw the adventurer's tiny sail,
Flit, stooping from the eastern gale;
And o'er these woods and waters broke
The cheer from Britain's hearts of oak,
As brightly on the voyager's eye,
Weary of forest, sea, and sky,
Breaking the dull continuous wood,
The Merrimac rolled down his flood;
Mingling that clear pellucid brook,
Which channels vast Agioochook
When spring–time's sun and shower unlock
The frozen fountains of the rock,
And more abundant waters given
From that pure lake, "The Smile of Heaven,"
Tributes from vale and mountain–side,—
With ocean's dark, eternal tide!

On yonder rocky cape, which braves
The stormy challenge of the waves,

Midst tangled vine and dwarfish wood,
The hardy Anglo–Saxon stood,
Planting upon the topmost crag
The staff of England's battle–flag;
And, while from out its heavy fold
Saint George's crimson cross unrolled,
Midst roll of drum and trumpet blare,
And weapons brandishing in air,
He gave to that lone promontory
The sweetest name in all his story;
Of her, the flower of Islam's daughters,
Whose harems look on Stamboul's waters,—
Who, when the chance of war had bound
The Moslem chain his limbs around,
Wreathed o'er with silk that iron chain,
Soothed with her smiles his hours of pain,
And fondly to her youthful slave
A dearer gift than freedom gave.

But look! the yellow light no more
Streams down on wave and verdant shore;
And clearly on the calm air swells
The twilight voice of distant bells.
From Ocean's bosom, white and thin,
The mists come slowly rolling in;
Hills, woods, the river's rocky rim,
Amidst the sea—like vapor swim,
While yonder lonely coast–light, set
Within its wave–washed minaret,
Half quenched, a beamless star and pale,
Shines dimly through its cloudy veil!

Home of my fathers!—I have stood
Where Hudson rolled his lordly flood
Seen sunrise rest and sunset fade
Along his frowning Palisade;
Looked down the Appalachian peak
On Juniata's silver streak;
Have seen along his valley gleam
The Mohawk's softly winding stream;
The level light of sunset shine
Through broad Potomac's hem of pine;
And autumn's rainbow–tinted banner
Hang lightly o'er the Susquehanna;
Yet wheresoe'er his step might be,
Thy wandering child looked back to thee!
Heard in his dreams thy river's sound
Of murmuring on its pebbly bound,
The unforgotten swell and roar
Of waves on thy familiar shore;
And saw, amidst the curtained gloom
And quiet of his lonely room,
Thy sunset scenes before him pass;
As, in Agrippa's magic glass,
The loved and lost arose to view,
Remembered groves in greenness grew,
Bathed still in childhood's morning dew,
Along whose bowers of beauty swept
Whatever Memory's mourners wept,
Sweet faces, which the charnel kept,
Young, gentle eyes, which long had slept;
And while the gazer leaned to trace,
More near, some dear familiar face,
He wept to find the vision flown,—
A phantom and a dream alone!
1841.

HAMPTON BEACH

The sunlight glitters keen and bright,
Where, miles away,
Lies stretching to my dazzled sight
A luminous belt, a misty light,
Beyond the dark pine bluffs and wastes of sandy gray.

The tremulous shadow of the Sea!
Against its ground
Of silvery light, rock, hill, and tree,
Still as a picture, clear and free,
With varying outline mark the coast for miles around.

On—on—we tread with loose–flung rein
Our seaward way,
Through dark–green fields and blossoming grain,
Where the wild brier–rose skirts the lane,
And bends above our heads the flowering locust spray.

Ha! like a kind hand on my brow
Comes this fresh breeze,
Cooling its dull and feverish glow,
While through my being seems to flow
The breath of a new life, the healing of the seas!

Now rest we, where this grassy mound
His feet hath set
In the great waters, which have bound
His granite ankles greenly round
With long and tangled moss, and weeds with cool spray wet.

Good—by to Pain and Care! I take
Mine ease to—day
Here where these sunny waters break,
And ripples this keen breeze, I shake
All burdens from the heart, all weary thoughts away.

I draw a freer breath, I seem
Like all I see—
Waves in the sun, the white—winged gleam
Of sea—birds in the slanting beam,
And far—off sails which flit before the south—wind free.

So when Time's veil shall fall asunder,
The soul may know
No fearful change, nor sudden wonder,
Nor sink the weight of mystery under,
But with the upward rise, and with the vastness grow.

And all we shrink from now may seem
No new revealing;
Familiar as our childhood's stream,

Or pleasant memory of a dream
The loved and cherished Past upon the new life stealing.

Serene and mild the untried light
May have its dawning;
And, as in summer's northern night
The evening and the dawn unite,
The sunset hues of Time blend with the soul's new morning.

I sit alone; in foam and spray
Wave after wave
Breaks on the rocks which, stern and gray,
Shoulder the broken tide away,
Or murmurs hoarse and strong through mossy cleft and cave.

What heed I of the dusty land
And noisy town?
I see the mighty deep expand
From its white line of glimmering sand
To where the blue of heaven on bluer waves shuts down!

In listless quietude of mind,
I yield to all
The change of cloud and wave and wind
And passive on the flood reclined,
I wander with the waves, and with them rise and fall.

But look, thou dreamer! wave and shore
In shadow lie;
The night—wind warns me back once more
To where, my native hill—tops o'er,
Bends like an arch of fire the glowing sunset sky.

So then, beach, bluff, and wave, farewell!
I bear with me
No token stone nor glittering shell,
But long and oft shall Memory tell
Of this brief thoughtful hour of musing by the Sea.
1843.

A DREAM OF SUMMER.

Bland as the morning breath of June
The southwest breezes play;
And, through its haze, the winter noon
Seems warm as summer's day.
The snow—plumed Angel of the North
Has dropped his icy spear;
Again the mossy earth looks forth,
Again the streams gush clear.

The fox his hillside cell forsakes,
The muskrat leaves his nook,
The bluebird in the meadow brakes
Is singing with the brook.

"Bear up, O Mother Nature!" cry
Bird, breeze, and streamlet free;
"Our winter voices prophesy
Of summer days to thee!"

So, in those winters of the soul,
By bitter blasts and drear
O'erswept from Memory's frozen pole,
Will sunny days appear.
Reviving Hope and Faith, they show
The soul its living powers,
And how beneath the winter's snow
Lie germs of summer flowers!

The Night is mother of the Day,
The Winter of the Spring,
And ever upon old Decay
The greenest mosses cling.
Behind the cloud the starlight lurks,
Through showers the sunbeams fall;
For God, who loveth all His works,
Has left His hope with all!
4th 1st month, 1847.

THE LAKESIDE

The shadows round the inland sea
Are deepening into night;

Slow up the slopes of Ossipee
They chase the lessening light.
Tired of the long day's blinding heat,
I rest my languid eye,
Lake of the Hills! where, cool and sweet,
Thy sunset waters lie!

Along the sky, in wavy lines,
O'er isle and reach and bay,
Green—belted with eternal pines,
The mountains stretch away.
Below, the maple masses sleep
Where shore with water blends,
While midway on the tranquil deep
The evening light descends.

So seemed it when yon hill's red crown,
Of old, the Indian trod,
And, through the sunset air, looked down
Upon the Smile of God.
To him of light and shade the laws
No forest skeptic taught;
Their living and eternal Cause
His truer instinct sought.

He saw these mountains in the light
Which now across them shines;
This lake, in summer sunset bright,
Walled round with sombering pines.
God near him seemed; from earth and skies

His loving voice he beard,
As, face to face, in Paradise,
Man stood before the Lord.

Thanks, O our Father! that, like him,
Thy tender love I see,
In radiant hill and woodland dim,
And tinted sunset sea.
For not in mockery dost Thou fill
Our earth with light and grace;
Thou hid'st no dark and cruel will
Behind Thy smiling face!
1849.

AUTUMN THOUGHTS

Gone hath the Spring, with all its flowers,
And gone the Summer's pomp and show,
And Autumn, in his leafless bowers,
Is waiting for the Winter's snow.

I said to Earth, so cold and gray,
"An emblem of myself thou art."
"Not so," the Earth did seem to say,
"For Spring shall warm my frozen heart."
I soothe my wintry sleep with dreams
Of warmer sun and softer rain,
And wait to hear the sound of streams
And songs of merry birds again.

But thou, from whom the Spring hath gone,
For whom the flowers no longer blow,
Who standest blighted and forlorn,
Like Autumn waiting for the snow;

No hope is thine of sunnier hours,
Thy Winter shall no more depart;
No Spring revive thy wasted flowers,
Nor Summer warm thy frozen heart.
1849.

ON RECEIVING AN EAGLE'S QUILL FROM LAKE SUPERIOR.

All day the darkness and the cold
Upon my heart have lain,
Like shadows on the winter sky,
Like frost upon the pane;

But now my torpid fancy wakes,
And, on thy Eagle's plume,
Rides forth, like Sindbad on his bird,
Or witch upon her broom!

Below me roar the rocking pines,
Before me spreads the lake
Whose long and solemn–sounding waves
Against the sunset break.

I hear the wild Rice–Eater thresh
The grain he has not sown;
I see, with flashing scythe of fire,
The prairie harvest mown!

I hear the far–off voyager's horn;
I see the Yankee's trail,—
His foot on every mountain–pass,
On every stream his sail.

By forest, lake, and waterfall,
I see his pedler show;
The mighty mingling with the mean,
The lofty with the low.

He's whittling by St. Mary's Falls,
Upon his loaded wain;
He's measuring o'er the Pictured Rocks,
With eager eyes of gain.

I hear the mattock in the mine,
The axe–stroke in the dell,
The clamor from the Indian lodge,
The Jesuit chapel bell!

I see the swarthy trappers come
From Mississippi's springs;
And war–chiefs with their painted brows,
And crests of eagle wings.

Behind the scared squaw's birch canoe,
The steamer smokes and raves;
And city lots are staked for sale
Above old Indian graves.

I hear the tread of pioneers
Of nations yet to be;
The first low wash of waves, where soon
Shall roll a human sea.

The rudiments of empire here
Are plastic yet and warm;
The chaos of a mighty world
Is rounding into form!

Each rude and jostling fragment soon
Its fitting place shall find,—
The raw material of a State,
Its muscle and its mind!

And, westering still, the star which leads
The New World in its train
Has tipped with fire the icy spears
Of many a mountain chain.

The snowy cones of Oregon
Are kindling on its way;
And California's golden sands
Gleam brighter in its ray!

Then blessings on thy eagle quill,
As, wandering far and wide,
I thank thee for this twilight dream
And Fancy's airy ride!

Yet, welcomer than regal plumes,
Which Western trappers find,
Thy free and pleasant thoughts, chance sown,
Like feathers on the wind.

Thy symbol be the mountain–bird,
Whose glistening quill I hold;
Thy home the ample air of hope,
And memory's sunset gold!

In thee, let joy with duty join,
And strength unite with love,
The eagle's pinions folding round
The warm heart of the dove!

So, when in darkness sleeps the vale
Where still the blind bird clings
The sunshine of the upper sky
Shall glitter on thy wings!
1849.

APRIL.

"The spring comes slowly up this way."
Christabel.

'T is the noon of the spring–time, yet never a bird
In the wind–shaken elm or the maple is heard;
For green meadow–grasses wide levels of snow,
And blowing of drifts where the crocus should blow;
Where wind–flower and violet, amber and white,
On south–sloping brooksides should smile in the light,

O'er the cold winter–beds of their late–waking roots
The frosty flake eddies, the ice–crystal shoots;
And, longing for light, under wind–driven heaps,
Round the boles of the pine–wood the ground–laurel creeps,
Unkissed of the sunshine, unbaptized of showers,
With buds scarcely swelled, which should burst into flowers
We wait for thy coming, sweet wind of the south!
For the touch of thy light wings, the kiss of thy mouth;
For the yearly evangel thou bearest from God,
Resurrection and life to the graves of the sod!
Up our long river–valley, for days, have not ceased
The wail and the shriek of the bitter northeast,
Raw and chill, as if winnowed through ices and snow,
All the way from the land of the wild Esquimau,
Until all our dreams of the land of the blest,
Like that red hunter's, turn to the sunny southwest.
O soul of the spring–time, its light and its breath,
Bring warmth to this coldness, bring life to this death;
Renew the great miracle; let us behold
The stone from the mouth of the sepulchre rolled,
And Nature, like Lazarus, rise, as of old!
Let our faith, which in darkness and coldness has lain,
Revive with the warmth and the brightness again,
And in blooming of flower and budding of tree
The symbols and types of our destiny see;
The life of the spring–time, the life of the whole,
And, as sun to the sleeping earth, love to the soul!
1852.

PICTURES

I.
Light, warmth, and sprouting greenness, and o'er all

Blue, stainless, steel–bright ether, raining down
Tranquillity upon the deep–hushed town,
The freshening meadows, and the hillsides brown;
Voice of the west–wind from the hills of pine,
And the brimmed river from its distant fall,
Low hum of bees, and joyous interlude
Of bird–songs in the streamlet–skirting wood,—
Heralds and prophecies of sound and sight,
Blessed forerunners of the warmth and light,
Attendant angels to the house of prayer,
With reverent footsteps keeping pace with mine,—
Once more, through God's great love, with you I share
A morn of resurrection sweet and fair
As that which saw, of old, in Palestine,
Immortal Love uprising in fresh bloom
From the dark night and winter of the tomb!
2d, 5th mo., 1852.

II.
White with its sun–bleached dust, the pathway winds
Before me; dust is on the shrunken grass,
And on the trees beneath whose boughs I pass;
Frail screen against the Hunter of the sky,
Who, glaring on me with his lidless eye,
While mounting with his dog–star high and higher
Ambushed in light intolerable, unbinds
The burnished quiver of his shafts of fire.
Between me and the hot fields of his South
A tremulous glow, as from a furnace–mouth,
Glimmers and swims before my dazzled sight,
As if the burning arrows of his ire
Broke as they fell, and shattered into light;
Yet on my cheek I feel the western wind,
And hear it telling to the orchard trees,

24

And to the faint and flower—forsaken bees,
Tales of fair meadows, green with constant streams,
And mountains rising blue and cool behind,
Where in moist dells the purple orchis gleams,
And starred with white the virgin's bower is twined.
So the o'erwearied pilgrim, as he fares
Along life's summer waste, at times is fanned,
Even at noontide, by the cool, sweet airs
Of a serener and a holier land,
Fresh as the morn, and as the dewfall bland.
Breath of the blessed Heaven for which we pray,
Blow from the eternal hills! make glad our earthly way!
8th mo., 1852.

SUMMER BY THE LAKESIDE

LAKE WINNIPESAUKEE.

I. NOON.
White clouds, whose shadows haunt the deep,
Light mists, whose soft embraces keep
The sunshine on the hills asleep!

O isles of calm! O dark, still wood!
And stiller skies that overbrood
Your rest with deeper quietude!

O shapes and hues, dim beckoning, through
Yon mountain gaps, my longing view
Beyond the purple and the blue,

To stiller sea and greener land,
And softer lights and airs more bland,
And skies,—the hollow of God's hand!

Transfused through you, O mountain friends!
With mine your solemn spirit blends,
And life no more hath separate ends.

I read each misty mountain sign,
I know the voice of wave and pine,
And I am yours, and ye are mine.

Life's burdens fall, its discords cease,
I lapse into the glad release
Of Nature's own exceeding peace.

O welcome calm of heart and mind!
As falls yon fir–tree's loosened rind
To leave a tenderer growth behind,

So fall the weary years away;
A child again, my head I lay
Upon the lap of this sweet day.

This western wind hath Lethean powers,
Yon noonday cloud nepenthe showers,
The lake is white with lotus–flowers!

Even Duty's voice is faint and low,
And slumberous Conscience, waking slow,
Forgets her blotted scroll to show.

The Shadow which pursues us all,
Whose ever–nearing steps appall,
Whose voice we hear behind us call,—

That Shadow blends with mountain gray,
It speaks but what the light waves say,—
Death walks apart from Fear to–day!

Rocked on her breast, these pines and I
Alike on Nature's love rely;
And equal seems to live or die.

Assured that He whose presence fills
With light the spaces of these hills
No evil to His creatures wills,

The simple faith remains, that He
Will do, whatever that may be,
The best alike for man and tree.

What mosses over one shall grow,
What light and life the other know,
Unanxious, leaving Him to show.

II. EVENING.
Yon mountain's side is black with night,
While, broad—orhed, o'er its gleaming crown
The moon, slow—rounding into sight,
On the hushed inland sea looks down.

How start to light the clustering isles,
Each silver—hemmed! How sharply show
The shadows of their rocky piles,
And tree—tops in the wave below!

How far and strange the mountains seem,

Dim—looming through the pale, still light
The vague, vast grouping of a dream,
They stretch into the solemn night.

Beneath, lake, wood, and peopled vale,
Hushed by that presence grand and grave,
Are silent, save the cricket's wail,
And low response of leaf and wave.

Fair scenes! whereto the Day and Night
Make rival love, I leave ye soon,
What time before the eastern light
The pale ghost of the setting moon

Shall hide behind yon rocky spines,
And the young archer, Morn, shall break
His arrows on the mountain pines,
And, golden—sandalled, walk the lake!

Farewell! around this smiling bay
Gay—hearted Health, and Life in bloom,
With lighter steps than mine, may stray
In radiant summers yet to come.

But none shall more regretful leave
These waters and these hills than I

Or, distant, fonder dream how eve
Or dawn is painting wave and sky;

How rising moons shine sad and mild
On wooded isle and silvering bay;
Or setting suns beyond the piled
And purple mountains lead the day;

Nor laughing girl, nor bearding boy,
Nor full−pulsed manhood, lingering here,
Shall add, to life's abounding joy,
The charmed repose to suffering dear.

Still waits kind Nature to impart
Her choicest gifts to such as gain
An entrance to her loving heart
Through the sharp discipline of pain.

Forever from the Hand that takes
One blessing from us others fall;
And, soon or late, our Father makes
His perfect recompense to all!

Oh, watched by Silence and the Night,
And folded in the strong embrace
Of the great mountains, with the light

Of the sweet heavens upon thy face,

Lake of the Northland! keep thy dower
Of beauty still, and while above
Thy solemn mountains speak of power,
Be thou the mirror of God's love.
1853.

THE FRUIT–GIFT.

Last night, just as the tints of autumn's sky
Of sunset faded from our hills and streams,
I sat, vague listening, lapped in twilight dreams,
To the leaf's rustle, and the cricket's cry.

Then, like that basket, flush with summer fruit,
Dropped by the angels at the Prophet's foot,
Came, unannounced, a gift of clustered sweetness,
Full–orbed, and glowing with the prisoned beams
Of summery suns, and rounded to completeness
By kisses of the south–wind and the dew.
Thrilled with a glad surprise, methought I knew
The pleasure of the homeward–turning Jew,
When Eshcol's clusters on his shoulders lay,
Dropping their sweetness on his desert way.

I said, "This fruit beseems no world of sin.

Its parent vine, rooted in Paradise,
O'ercrept the wall, and never paid the price
Of the great mischief,—an ambrosial tree,
Eden's exotic, somehow smuggled in,
To keep the thorns and thistles company."
Perchance our frail, sad mother plucked in haste
A single vine—slip as she passed the gate,
Where the dread sword alternate paled and burned,
And the stern angel, pitying her fate,
Forgave the lovely trespasser, and turned
Aside his face of fire; and thus the waste
And fallen world hath yet its annual taste
Of primal good, to prove of sin the cost,
And show by one gleaned ear the mighty harvest lost.
1854.

FLOWERS IN WINTER

PAINTED UPON A PORTE LIVRE.

How strange to greet, this frosty morn,
In graceful counterfeit of flowers,
These children of the meadows, born
Of sunshine and of showers!

How well the conscious wood retains
The pictures of its flower—sown home,
The lights and shades, the purple stains,
And golden hues of bloom!

It was a happy thought to bring
To the dark season's frost and rime
This painted memory of spring,
This dream of summer–time.

Our hearts are lighter for its sake,
Our fancy's age renews its youth,
And dim–remembered fictions take
The guise of—present truth.

A wizard of the Merrimac,—
So old ancestral legends say,
Could call green leaf and blossom back
To frosted stem and spray.

The dry logs of the cottage wall,
Beneath his touch, put out their leaves
The clay–bound swallow, at his call,
Played round the icy eaves.

The settler saw his oaken flail
Take bud, and bloom before his eyes;
From frozen pools he saw the pale,
Sweet summer lilies rise.

To their old homes, by man profaned,
Came the sad dryads, exiled long,
And through their leafy tongues complained
Of household use and wrong.

The beechen platter sprouted wild,
The pipkin wore its old–time green
The cradle o'er the sleeping child
Became a leafy screen.

Haply our gentle friend hath met,
While wandering in her sylvan quest,
Haunting his native woodlands yet,
That Druid of the West;

And, while the dew on leaf and flower
Glistened in moonlight clear and still,
Learned the dusk wizard's spell of power,
And caught his trick of skill.

But welcome, be it new or old,
The gift which makes the day more bright,
And paints, upon the ground of cold
And darkness, warmth and light.

Without is neither gold nor green;
Within, for birds, the birch–logs sing;
Yet, summer–like, we sit between
The autumn and the spring.

The one, with bridal blush of rose,
And sweetest breath of woodland balm,
And one whose matron lips unclose
In smiles of saintly calm.

Fill soft and deep, O winter snow!
The sweet azalea's oaken dells,
And hide the bank where roses blow,
And swing the azure bells!

O'erlay the amber violet's leaves,
The purple aster's brookside home,
Guard all the flowers her pencil gives
A life beyond their bloom.

And she, when spring comes round again,
By greening slope and singing flood
Shall wander, seeking, not in vain,
Her darlings of the wood.
1855.

THE MAYFLOWERS

The trailing arbutus, or mayflower, grows abundantly in the vicinity of Plymouth, and was the first flower that greeted the Pilgrims after their fearful winter. The name mayflower was familiar in England, as the application of it to the historic vessel shows, but it was applied by the English, and still is, to the hawthorn. Its use in New England in connection with *Epigma repens dates from a very early day, some claiming that the first Pilgrims so used it, in affectionate memory of the vessel and its English flower association.*

Sad Mayflower! watched by winter stars,
And nursed by winter gales,
With petals of the sleeted spars,
And leaves of frozen sails!

What had she in those dreary hours,
Within her ice–rimmed bay,
In common with the wild–wood flowers,
The first sweet smiles of May?

Yet, "God be praised!" the Pilgrim said,
Who saw the blossoms peer
Above the brown leaves, dry and dead,
"Behold our Mayflower here!"

"God wills it: here our rest shall be,
Our years of wandering o'er;
For us the Mayflower of the sea
Shall spread her sails no more."

O sacred flowers of faith and hope,
As sweetly now as then
Ye bloom on many a birchen slope,
In many a pine–dark glen.

Behind the sea–wall's rugged length,
Unchanged, your leaves unfold,
Like love behind the manly strength
Of the brave hearts of old.

So live the fathers in their sons,
Their sturdy faith be ours,
And ours the love that overruns
Its rocky strength with flowers!

The Pilgrim's wild and wintry day
Its shadow round us draws;
The Mayflower of his stormy bay,
Our Freedom's struggling cause.

But warmer suns erelong shall bring
To life the frozen sod;
And through dead leaves of hope shall spring
Afresh the flowers of God!
1856.

THE LAST WALK IN AUTUMN.

I.

O'er the bare woods, whose outstretched hands
Plead with the leaden heavens in vain,
I see, beyond the valley lands,
The sea's long level dim with rain.
Around me all things, stark and dumb,
Seem praying for the snows to come,
And, for the summer bloom and greenness gone,
With winter's sunset lights and dazzling morn atone.

II.

Along the river's summer walk,
The withered tufts of asters nod;
And trembles on its arid stalk
The boar plume of the golden-rod.
And on a ground of sombre fir,
And azure-studded juniper,
The silver birch its buds of purple shows,
And scarlet berries tell where bloomed the sweet wild-rose!

III.

With mingled sound of horns and bells,
A far–heard clang, the wild geese fly,
Storm–sent, from Arctic moors and fells,
Like a great arrow through the sky,
Two dusky lines converged in one,
Chasing the southward–flying sun;
While the brave snow–bird and the hardy jay
Call to them from the pines, as if to bid them stay.

IV.

I passed this way a year ago
The wind blew south; the noon of day
Was warm as June's; and save that snow
Flecked the low mountains far away,
And that the vernal–seeming breeze
Mocked faded grass and leafless trees,
I might have dreamed of summer as I lay,
Watching the fallen leaves with the soft wind at play.

V.

Since then, the winter blasts have piled
The white pagodas of the snow
On these rough slopes, and, strong and wild,
Yon river, in its overflow
Of spring–time rain and sun, set free,
Crashed with its ices to the sea;
And over these gray fields, then green and gold,
The summer corn has waved, the thunder's organ rolled.

VI.

Rich gift of God! A year of time
What pomp of rise and shut of day,
What hues wherewith our Northern clime
Makes autumn's dropping woodlands gay,
What airs outblown from ferny dells,
And clover—bloom and sweetbrier smells,
What songs of brooks and birds, what fruits and flowers,
Green woods and moonlit snows, have in its round been ours!

VII.

I know not how, in other lands,
The changing seasons come and go;
What splendors fall on Syrian sands,
What purple lights on Alpine snow!
Nor how the pomp of sunrise waits
On Venice at her watery gates;
A dream alone to me is Arno's vale,
And the Alhambra's halls are but a traveller's tale.

VIII.

Yet, on life's current, he who drifts
Is one with him who rows or sails
And he who wanders widest lifts
No more of beauty's jealous veils
Than he who from his doorway sees
The miracle of flowers and trees,
Feels the warm Orient in the noonday air,
And from cloud minarets hears the sunset call to prayer!

IX.

The eye may well be glad that looks
Where Pharpar's fountains rise and fall;
But he who sees his native brooks
Laugh in the sun, has seen them all.
The marble palaces of Ind
Rise round him in the snow and wind;
From his lone sweetbrier Persian Hafiz smiles,
And Rome's cathedral awe is in his woodland aisles.

X.

And thus it is my fancy blends
The near at hand and far and rare;
And while the same horizon bends
Above the silver–sprinkled hair
Which flashed the light of morning skies
On childhood's wonder–lifted eyes,
Within its round of sea and sky and field,
Earth wheels with all her zones, the Kosmos stands revealed.

XI.

And thus the sick man on his bed,
The toiler to his task–work bound,
Behold their prison–walls outspread,
Their clipped horizon widen round!
While freedom–giving fancy waits,
Like Peter's angel at the gates,
The power is theirs to baffle care and pain,
To bring the lost world back, and make it theirs again!

XII.
What lack of goodly company,
When masters of the ancient lyre
Obey my call, and trace for me
Their words of mingled tears and fire!
I talk with Bacon, grave and wise,
I read the world with Pascal's eyes;
And priest and sage, with solemn brows austere,
And poets, garland–bound, the Lords of Thought, draw near.

XIII.
Methinks, O friend, I hear thee say,
   "In vain the human heart we mock;
Bring living guests who love the day,
Not ghosts who fly at crow of cock!
The herbs we share with flesh and blood
Are better than ambrosial food
With laurelled shades." I grant it, nothing loath,
But doubly blest is he who can partake of both.

XIV.
He who might Plato's banquet grace,
Have I not seen before me sit,
And watched his puritanic face,
With more than Eastern wisdom lit?
Shrewd mystic! who, upon the back
Of his Poor Richard's Almanac,
Writing the Sufi's song, the Gentoo's dream,
Links Manu's age of thought to Fulton's age of steam!

XV.

Here too, of answering love secure,
Have I not welcomed to my hearth
The gentle pilgrim troubadour,
Whose songs have girdled half the earth;
Whose pages, like the magic mat
Whereon the Eastern lover sat,
Have borne me over Rhine—land's purple vines,
And Nubia's tawny sands, and Phrygia's mountain pines!

XVI.

And he, who to the lettered wealth
Of ages adds the lore unpriced,
The wisdom and the moral health,
The ethics of the school of Christ;
The statesman to his holy trust,
As the Athenian archon, just,
Struck down, exiled like him for truth alone,
Has he not graced my home with beauty all his own?

XVII.

What greetings smile, what farewells wave,
What loved ones enter and depart!
The good, the beautiful, the brave,
The Heaven—lent treasures of the heart!
How conscious seems the frozen sod
And beechen slope whereon they trod
The oak—leaves rustle, and the dry grass bends
Beneath the shadowy feet of lost or absent friends.

XVIII.
Then ask not why to these bleak hills
I cling, as clings the tufted moss,
To bear the winter's lingering chills,
The mocking spring's perpetual loss.
I dream of lands where summer smiles,
And soft winds blow from spicy isles,
But scarce would Ceylon's breath of flowers be sweet,
Could I not feel thy soil, New England, at my feet!

XIX.
At times I long for gentler skies,
And bathe in dreams of softer air,
But homesick tears would fill the eyes
That saw the Cross without the Bear.
The pine must whisper to the palm,
The north−wind break the tropic calm;
And with the dreamy languor of the Line,
The North's keen virtue blend, and strength to beauty join.

XX.
Better to stem with heart and hand
The roaring tide of life, than lie,
Unmindful, on its flowery strand,
Of God's occasions drifting by
Better with naked nerve to bear
The needles of this goading air,
Than, in the lap of sensual ease, forego
The godlike power to do, the godlike aim to know.

XXI.
Home of my heart! to me more fair
Than gay Versailles or Windsor's halls,
The painted, shingly town–house where
The freeman's vote for Freedom falls!
The simple roof where prayer is made,
Than Gothic groin and colonnade;
The living temple of the heart of man,
Than Rome's sky–mocking vault, or many–spired Milan!

XXII.
More dear thy equal village schools,
Where rich and poor the Bible read,
Than classic halls where Priestcraft rules,
And Learning wears the chains of Creed;
Thy glad Thanksgiving, gathering in
The scattered sheaves of home and kin,
Than the mad license ushering Lenten pains,
Or holidays of slaves who laugh and dance in chains.

XXIII.
And sweet homes nestle in these dales,
And perch along these wooded swells;
And, blest beyond Arcadian vales,
They hear the sound of Sabbath bells!
Here dwells no perfect man sublime,
Nor woman winged before her time,
But with the faults and follies of the race,
Old home–bred virtues hold their not unhonored place.

XXIV.
Here manhood struggles for the sake
Of mother, sister, daughter, wife,
The graces and the loves which make
The music of the march of life;
And woman, in her daily round
Of duty, walks on holy ground.
No unpaid menial tills the soil, nor here
Is the bad lesson learned at human rights to sneer.

XXV.
Then let the icy north—wind blow
The trumpets of the coming storm,
To arrowy sleet and blinding snow
Yon slanting lines of rain transform.
Young hearts shall hail the drifted cold,
As gayly as I did of old;
And I, who watch them through the frosty pane,
Unenvious, live in them my boyhood o'er again.

XXVI.
And I will trust that He who heeds
The life that hides in mead and wold,
Who hangs yon alder's crimson beads,
And stains these mosses green and gold,
Will still, as He hath done, incline
His gracious care to me and mine;
Grant what we ask aright, from wrong debar,
And, as the earth grows dark, make brighter every star!

XXVII.
I have not seen, I may not see,
My hopes for man take form in fact,
But God will give the victory
In due time; in that faith I act.
And lie who sees the future sure,
The baffling present may endure,
And bless, meanwhile, the unseen Hand that leads
The heart's desires beyond the halting step of deeds.

XXVIII.
And thou, my song, I send thee forth,
Where harsher songs of mine have flown;
Go, find a place at home and hearth
Where'er thy singer's name is known;
Revive for him the kindly thought
Of friends; and they who love him not,
Touched by some strain of thine, perchance may take
The hand he proffers all, and thank him for thy sake.
1857.

THE FIRST FLOWERS

For ages on our river borders,
These tassels in their tawny bloom,
And willowy studs of downy silver,
Have prophesied of Spring to come.

For ages have the unbound waters
Smiled on them from their pebbly hem,
And the clear carol of the robin
And song of bluebird welcomed them.

But never yet from smiling river,
Or song of early bird, have they
Been greeted with a gladder welcome
Than whispers from my heart to–day.

They break the spell of cold and darkness,
The weary watch of sleepless pain;
And from my heart, as from the river,
The ice of winter melts again.

Thanks, Mary! for this wild–wood token
Of Freya's footsteps drawing near;
Almost, as in the rune of Asgard,
The growing of the grass I hear.

It is as if the pine–trees called me
From ceiled room and silent books,
To see the dance of woodland shadows,
And hear the song of April brooks!

As in the old Teutonic ballad
Of Odenwald live bird and tree,
Together live in bloom and music,
I blend in song thy flowers and thee.

Earth's rocky tablets bear forever
The dint of rain and small bird's track
Who knows but that my idle verses
May leave some trace by Merrimac!

The bird that trod the mellow layers
Of the young earth is sought in vain;
The cloud is gone that wove the sandstone,
From God's design, with threads of rain!

So, when this fluid age we live in
Shall stiffen round my careless rhyme,
Who made the vagrant tracks may puzzle
The savants of the coming time;

And, following out their dim suggestions,
Some idly–curious hand may draw
My doubtful portraiture, as Cuvier
Drew fish and bird from fin and claw.

And maidens in the far–off twilights,
Singing my words to breeze and stream,
Shall wonder if the old–time Mary
Were real, or the rhymer's dream!
1st 3d mo., 1857.

THE OLD BURYING–GROUND.

Our vales are sweet with fern and rose,
Our hills are maple–crowned;
But not from them our fathers chose
The village burying–ground.

The dreariest spot in all the land
To Death they set apart;
With scanty grace from Nature's hand,
And none from that of Art.

A winding wall of mossy stone,
Frost–flung and broken, lines
A lonesome acre thinly grown
With grass and wandering vines.

Without the wall a birch–tree shows
Its drooped and tasselled head;
Within, a stag–horned sumach grows,

Fern—leafed, with spikes of red.

There, sheep that graze the neighboring plain
Like white ghosts come and go,
The farm—horse drags his fetlock chain,
The cow—bell tinkles slow.

Low moans the river from its bed,
The distant pines reply;
Like mourners shrinking from the dead,
They stand apart and sigh.

Unshaded smites the summer sun,
Unchecked the winter blast;
The school—girl learns the place to shun,
With glances backward cast.

For thus our fathers testified,
That he might read who ran,
The emptiness of human pride,
The nothingness of man.

They dared not plant the grave with flowers,
Nor dress the funeral sod,
Where, with a love as deep as ours,
They left their dead with God.

The hard and thorny path they kept
From beauty turned aside;
Nor missed they over those who slept
The grace to life denied.

Yet still the wilding flowers would blow,
The golden leaves would fall,
The seasons come, the seasons go,
And God be good to all.

Above the graves the' blackberry hung
In bloom and green its wreath,
And harebells swung as if they rung
The chimes of peace beneath.

The beauty Nature loves to share,
The gifts she hath for all,
The common light, the common air,
O'ercrept the graveyard's wall.

It knew the glow of eventide,
The sunrise and the noon,
And glorified and sanctified
It slept beneath the moon.

With flowers or snow—flakes for its sod,
Around the seasons ran,
And evermore the love of God
Rebuked the fear of man.

We dwell with fears on either hand,
Within a daily strife,
And spectral problems waiting stand
Before the gates of life.

The doubts we vainly seek to solve,
The truths we know, are one;
The known and nameless stars revolve
Around the Central Sun.

And if we reap as we have sown,
And take the dole we deal,
The law of pain is love alone,
The wounding is to heal.

Unharmed from change to change we glide,
We fall as in our dreams;
The far—off terror at our side
A smiling angel seems.

Secure on God's all—tender heart
Alike rest great and small;
Why fear to lose our little part,
When He is pledged for all?

O fearful heart and troubled brain
Take hope and strength from this,—
That Nature never hints in vain,
Nor prophesies amiss.

Her wild birds sing the same sweet stave,
Her lights and airs are given
Alike to playground and the grave;
And over both is Heaven.
1858

THE PALM—TREE.

Is it the palm, the cocoa—palm,
On the Indian Sea, by the isles of balm?
Or is it a ship in the breezeless calm?

A ship whose keel is of palm beneath,
Whose ribs of palm have a palm—bark sheath,
And a rudder of palm it steereth with.

Branches of palm are its spars and rails,
Fibres of palm are its woven sails,
And the rope is of palm that idly trails!

What does the good ship bear so well?
The cocoa–nut with its stony shell,
And the milky sap of its inner cell.

What are its jars, so smooth and fine,
But hollowed nuts, filled with oil and wine,
And the cabbage that ripens under the Line?

Who smokes his nargileh, cool and calm?
The master, whose cunning and skill could charm
Cargo and ship from the bounteous palm.

In the cabin he sits on a palm–mat soft,
From a beaker of palm his drink is quaffed,
And a palm–thatch shields from the sun aloft!

His dress is woven of palmy strands,
And he holds a palm–leaf scroll in his hands,
Traced with the Prophet's wise commands!

The turban folded about his head
Was daintily wrought of the palm–leaf braid,
And the fan that cools him of palm was made.

Of threads of palm was the carpet spun
Whereon he kneels when the day is done,
And the foreheads of Islam are bowed as one!

To him the palm is a gift divine,
Wherein all uses of man combine,—
House, and raiment, and food, and wine!

And, in the hour of his great release,
His need of the palm shall only cease
With the shroud wherein he lieth in peace.

"Allah il Allah!" he sings his psalm,
On the Indian Sea, by the isles of balm;
"Thanks to Allah who gives the palm!"
1858.

THE RIVER PATH.

No bird–song floated down the hill,

The tangled bank below was still;

No rustle from the birchen stem,
No ripple from the water's hem.

The dusk of twilight round us grew,
We felt the falling of the dew;

For, from us, ere the day was done,
The wooded hills shut out the sun.

But on the river's farther side
We saw the hill–tops glorified,—

A tender glow, exceeding fair,
A dream of day without its glare.

With us the damp, the chill, the gloom
With them the sunset's rosy bloom;

While dark, through willowy vistas seen,
The river rolled in shade between.

From out the darkness where we trod,
We gazed upon those bills of God,

Whose light seemed not of moon or sun.
We spake not, but our thought was one.

We paused, as if from that bright shore
Beckoned our dear ones gone before;

And stilled our beating hearts to hear
The voices lost to mortal ear!

Sudden our pathway turned from night;
The hills swung open to the light;

Through their green gates the sunshine showed,
A long, slant splendor downward flowed.

Down glade and glen and bank it rolled;
It bridged the shaded stream with gold;

And, borne on piers of mist, allied
The shadowy with the sunlit side!

"So," prayed we, "when our feet draw near
The river dark, with mortal fear,

"And the night cometh chill with dew,
O Father! let Thy light break through!

"So let the hills of doubt divide,
So bridge with faith the sunless tide!

"So let the eyes that fail on earth
On Thy eternal hills look forth;

"And in Thy beckoning angels know
The dear ones whom we loved below!"
1880.

MOUNTAIN PICTURES.

I. FRANCONIA FROM THE PEMIGEWASSET

Once more, O Mountains of the North, unveil
Your brows, and lay your cloudy mantles by
And once more, ere the eyes that seek ye fail,
Uplift against the blue walls of the sky
Your mighty shapes, and let the sunshine weave
Its golden net—work in your belting woods,
Smile down in rainbows from your falling floods,
And on your kingly brows at morn and eve
Set crowns of fire! So shall my soul receive
Haply the secret of your calm and strength,
Your unforgotten beauty interfuse
My common life, your glorious shapes and hues
And sun—dropped splendors at my bidding come,
Loom vast through dreams, and stretch in billowy length
From the sea—level of my lowland home!

They rise before me! Last night's thunder—gust
Roared not in vain: for where its lightnings thrust
Their tongues of fire, the great peaks seem so near,
Burned clean of mist, so starkly bold and clear,
I almost pause the wind in the pines to hear,
The loose rock's fall, the steps of browsing deer.
The clouds that shattered on yon slide—worn walls
And splintered on the rocks their spears of rain
Have set in play a thousand waterfalls,
Making the dusk and silence of the woods
Glad with the laughter of the chasing floods,
And luminous with blown spray and silver gleams,
While, in the vales below, the dry—lipped streams
Sing to the freshened meadow—lands again.
So, let me hope, the battle—storm that beats
The land with hail and fire may pass away
With its spent thunders at the break of day,
Like last night's clouds, and leave, as it retreats,

A greener earth and fairer sky behind,
Blown crystal—clear by Freedom's Northern wind!

II. MONADNOCK FROM WACHUSET.

I would I were a painter, for the sake
Of a sweet picture, and of her who led,
A fitting guide, with reverential tread,
Into that mountain mystery. First a lake
Tinted with sunset; next the wavy lines
Of far receding hills; and yet more far,
Monadnock lifting from his night of pines
His rosy forehead to the evening star.
Beside us, purple—zoned, Wachuset laid
His head against the West, whose warm light made
His aureole; and o'er him, sharp and clear,
Like a shaft of lightning in mid—launching stayed,
A single level cloud—line, shone upon
By the fierce glances of the sunken sun,
Menaced the darkness with its golden spear!

So twilight deepened round us. Still and black
The great woods climbed the mountain at our back;
And on their skirts, where yet the lingering day
On the shorn greenness of the clearing lay,
The brown old farm—house like a bird's—nest hung.
With home—life sounds the desert air was stirred
The bleat of sheep along the hill we heard,
The bucket plashing in the cool, sweet well,
The pasture—bars that clattered as they fell;
Dogs barked, fowls fluttered, cattle lowed; the gate
Of the barn—yard creaked beneath the merry weight
Of sun—brown children, listening, while they swung,

The welcome sound of supper–call to hear;
And down the shadowy lane, in tinklings clear,
The pastoral curfew of the cow–bell rung.
Thus soothed and pleased, our backward path we took,
Praising the farmer's home. He only spake,
Looking into the sunset o'er the lake,
Like one to whom the far–off is most near:
"Yes, most folks think it has a pleasant look;
I love it for my good old mother's sake,
Who lived and died here in the peace of God!"
The lesson of his words we pondered o'er,
As silently we turned the eastern flank
Of the mountain, where its shadow deepest sank,
Doubling the night along our rugged road:
We felt that man was more than his abode,—
The inward life than Nature's raiment more;
And the warm sky, the sundown–tinted hill,
The forest and the lake, seemed dwarfed and dim
Before the saintly soul, whose human will
Meekly in the Eternal footsteps trod,
Making her homely toil and household ways
An earthly echo of the song of praise
Swelling from angel lips and harps of seraphim.
1862.

THE VANISHERS.

Sweetest of all childlike dreams
In the simple Indian lore
Still to me the legend seems
Of the shapes who flit before.

Flitting, passing, seen and gone,
Never reached nor found at rest,
Baffling search, but beckoning on
To the Sunset of the Blest.

From the clefts of mountain rocks,
Through the dark of lowland firs,
Flash the eyes and flow the locks
Of the mystic Vanishers!

And the fisher in his skiff,
And the hunter on the moss,
Hear their call from cape and cliff,
See their hands the birch–leaves toss.

Wistful, longing, through the green
Twilight of the clustered pines,
In their faces rarely seen
Beauty more than mortal shines.

Fringed with gold their mantles flow
On the slopes of westering knolls;
In the wind they whisper low
Of the Sunset Land of Souls.

Doubt who may, O friend of mine!
Thou and I have seen them too;
On before with beck and sign
Still they glide, and we pursue.

More than clouds of purple trail
In the gold of setting day;
More than gleams of wing or sail
Beckon from the sea–mist gray.

Glimpses of immortal youth,
Gleams and glories seen and flown,
Far–heard voices sweet with truth,
Airs from viewless Eden blown;

Beauty that eludes our grasp,
Sweetness that transcends our taste,
Loving hands we may not clasp,
Shining feet that mock our haste;

Gentle eyes we closed below,
Tender voices heard once more,
Smile and call us, as they go
On and onward, still before.

Guided thus, O friend of mine
Let us walk our little way,
Knowing by each beckoning sign
That we are not quite astray.

Chase we still, with baffled feet,
Smiling eye and waving hand,
Sought and seeker soon shall meet,
Lost and found, in Sunset Land
1864.

THE PAGEANT.

A sound as if from bells of silver,
Or elfin cymbals smitten clear,
Through the frost–pictured panes I hear.

A brightness which outshines the morning,
A splendor brooking no delay,
Beckons and tempts my feet away.

I leave the trodden village highway
For virgin snow–paths glimmering through
A jewelled elm–tree avenue;

Where, keen against the walls of sapphire,
The gleaming tree–bolls, ice–embossed,
Hold up their chandeliers of frost.

I tread in Orient halls enchanted,
I dream the Saga's dream of caves
Gem–lit beneath the North Sea waves!

I walk the land of Eldorado,
I touch its mimic garden bowers,
Its silver leaves and diamond flowers!

The flora of the mystic mine–world
Around me lifts on crystal stems
The petals of its clustered gems!

What miracle of weird transforming
In this wild work of frost and light,
This glimpse of glory infinite!

This foregleam of the Holy City
Like that to him of Patmos given,
The white bride coming down from heaven!

How flash the ranked and mail–clad alders,
Through what sharp–glancing spears of reeds
The brook its muffled water leads!

Yon maple, like the bush of Horeb,
Burns unconsumed: a white, cold fire
Rays out from every grassy spire.

Each slender rush and spike of mullein,
Low laurel shrub and drooping fern,
Transfigured, blaze where'er I turn.

How yonder Ethiopian hemlock
Crowned with his glistening circlet stands!
What jewels light his swarthy hands!

Here, where the forest opens southward,
Between its hospitable pines,
As through a door, the warm sun shines.

The jewels loosen on the branches,
And lightly, as the soft winds blow,
Fall, tinkling, on the ice below.

And through the clashing of their cymbals
I hear the old familiar fall
Of water down the rocky wall,

Where, from its wintry prison breaking,
In dark and silence hidden long,
The brook repeats its summer song.

One instant flashing in the sunshine,
Keen as a sabre from its sheath,
Then lost again the ice beneath.

I hear the rabbit lightly leaping,
The foolish screaming of the jay,
The chopper's axe–stroke far away;

The clamor of some neighboring barn–yard,
The lazy cock's belated crow,
Or cattle–tramp in crispy snow.

And, as in some enchanted forest
The lost knight hears his comrades sing,
And, near at hand, their bridles ring,—

So welcome I these sounds and voices,
These airs from far—off summer blown,
This life that leaves me not alone.

For the white glory overawes me;
The crystal terror of the seer
Of Chebar's vision blinds me here.

Rebuke me not, O sapphire heaven!
Thou stainless earth, lay not on me,
Thy keen reproach of purity,

If, in this August presence—chamber,
I sigh for summer's leaf—green gloom
And warm airs thick with odorous bloom!

Let the strange frost—work sink and crumble,
And let the loosened tree—boughs swing,
Till all their bells of silver ring.

Shine warmly down, thou sun of noontime,
On this chill pageant, melt and move
The winter's frozen heart with love.

And, soft and low, thou wind south—blowing,
Breathe through a veil of tenderest haze
Thy prophecy of summer days.

Come with thy green relief of promise,
And to this dead, cold splendor bring
The living jewels of the spring!
1869.

THE PRESSED GENTIAN.

The time of gifts has come again,
And, on my northern window—pane,
Outlined against the day's brief light,
A Christmas token hangs in sight.

The wayside travellers, as they pass,
Mark the gray disk of clouded glass;
And the dull blankness seems, perchance,
Folly to their wise ignorance.

They cannot from their outlook see
The perfect grace it hath for me;
For there the flower, whose fringes through
The frosty breath of autumn blew,
Turns from without its face of bloom

To the warm tropic of my room,
As fair as when beside its brook
The hue of bending skies it took.

So from the trodden ways of earth,
Seem some sweet souls who veil their worth,
And offer to the careless glance
The clouding gray of circumstance.
They blossom best where hearth—fires burn,
To loving eyes alone they turn
The flowers of inward grace, that hide
Their beauty from the world outside.

But deeper meanings come to me,
My half—immortal flower, from thee!
Man judges from a partial view,
None ever yet his brother knew;
The Eternal Eye that sees the whole
May better read the darkened soul,
And find, to outward sense denied,
The flower upon its inmost side
1872.

A MYSTERY.

The river hemmed with leaning trees
Wound through its meadows green;
A low, blue line of mountains showed
The open pines between.

One sharp, tall peak above them all
Clear into sunlight sprang
I saw the river of my dreams,
The mountains that I sang!

No clue of memory led me on,
But well the ways I knew;
A feeling of familiar things
With every footstep grew.

Not otherwise above its crag
Could lean the blasted pine;
Not otherwise the maple hold
Aloft its red ensign.

So up the long and shorn foot–hills
The mountain road should creep;
So, green and low, the meadow fold
Its red–haired kine asleep.

The river wound as it should wind;
Their place the mountains took;
The white torn fringes of their clouds
Wore no unwonted look.

Yet ne'er before that river's rim
Was pressed by feet of mine,
Never before mine eyes had crossed
That broken mountain line.

A presence, strange at once and known,
Walked with me as my guide;
The skirts of some forgotten life
Trailed noiseless at my side.

Was it a dim–remembered dream?
Or glimpse through ions old?
The secret which the mountains kept
The river never told.

But from the vision ere it passed
A tender hope I drew,
And, pleasant as a dawn of spring,
The thought within me grew,

That love would temper every change,
And soften all surprise,
And, misty with the dreams of earth,
The hills of Heaven arise.
1873.

A SEA DREAM.

We saw the slow tides go and come,
The curving surf–lines lightly drawn,
The gray rocks touched with tender bloom
Beneath the fresh–blown rose of dawn.

We saw in richer sunsets lost
The sombre pomp of showery noons;
And signalled spectral sails that crossed
The weird, low light of rising moons.

On stormy eves from cliff and head
We saw the white spray tossed and spurned;
While over all, in gold and red,
Its face of fire the lighthouse turned.

The rail–car brought its daily crowds,
Half curious, half indifferent,
Like passing sails or floating clouds,
We saw them as they came and went.

But, one calm morning, as we lay
And watched the mirage–lifted wall
Of coast, across the dreamy bay,

And heard afar the curlew call,

And nearer voices, wild or tame,
Of airy flock and childish throng,
Up from the water's edge there came
Faint snatches of familiar song.

Careless we heard the singer's choice
Of old and common airs; at last
The tender pathos of his voice
In one low chanson held us fast.

A song that mingled joy and pain,
And memories old and sadly sweet;
While, timing to its minor strain,
The waves in lapsing cadence beat.

. . . . .

The waves are glad in breeze and sun;
The rocks are fringed with foam;
I walk once more a haunted shore,
A stranger, yet at home,
A land of dreams I roam.

Is this the wind, the soft sea wind
That stirred thy locks of brown?
Are these the rocks whose mosses knew
The trail of thy light gown,
Where boy and girl sat down?

I see the gray fort's broken wall,
The boats that rock below;
And, out at sea, the passing sails
We saw so long ago
Rose–red in morning's glow.

The freshness of the early time
On every breeze is blown;
As glad the sea, as blue the sky,—
The change is ours alone;
The saddest is my own.

A stranger now, a world–worn man,
Is he who bears my name;
But thou, methinks, whose mortal life
Immortal youth became,
Art evermore the same.

Thou art not here, thou art not there,
Thy place I cannot see;
I only know that where thou art

The blessed angels be,
And heaven is glad for thee.

Forgive me if the evil years
Have left on me their sign;
Wash out, O soul so beautiful,
The many stains of mine
In tears of love divine!

I could not look on thee and live,
If thou wert by my side;
The vision of a shining one,
The white and heavenly bride,
Is well to me denied.

But turn to me thy dear girl–face
Without the angel's crown,
The wedded roses of thy lips,
Thy loose hair rippling down
In waves of golden brown.

Look forth once more through space and time,
And let thy sweet shade fall
In tenderest grace of soul and form
On memory's frescoed wall,
A shadow, and yet all!

Draw near, more near, forever dear!
Where'er I rest or roam,
Or in the city's crowded streets,
Or by the blown sea foam,
The thought of thee is home!

. . . . .

At breakfast hour the singer read
The city news, with comment wise,
Like one who felt the pulse of trade
Beneath his finger fall and rise.

His look, his air, his curt speech, told
The man of action, not of books,
To whom the corners made in gold
And stocks were more than seaside nooks.

Of life beneath the life confessed
His song had hinted unawares;
Of flowers in traffic's ledgers pressed,
Of human hearts in bulls and bears.

But eyes in vain were turned to watch
That face so hard and shrewd and strong;
And ears in vain grew sharp to catch

The meaning of that morning song.

In vain some sweet–voiced querist sought
To sound him, leaving as she came;
Her baited album only caught
A common, unromantic name.

No word betrayed the mystery fine,
That trembled on the singer's tongue;
He came and went, and left no sign
Behind him save the song he sung.
1874.

HAZEL BLOSSOMS.

The summer warmth has left the sky,
The summer songs have died away;
And, withered, in the footpaths lie
The fallen leaves, but yesterday
With ruby and with topaz gay.

The grass is browning on the hills;
No pale, belated flowers recall
The astral fringes of the rills,
And drearily the dead vines fall,
Frost–blackened, from the roadside wall.

Yet through the gray and sombre wood,
Against the dusk of fir and pine,
Last of their floral sisterhood,
The hazel's yellow blossoms shine,
The tawny gold of Afric's mine!

Small beauty hath my unsung flower,
For spring to own or summer hail;
But, in the season's saddest hour,
To skies that weep and winds that wail
Its glad surprisals never fail.

O days grown cold! O life grown old
No rose of June may bloom again;
But, like the hazel's twisted gold,
Through early frost and latter rain
Shall hints of summer–time remain.

And as within the hazel's bough
A gift of mystic virtue dwells,
That points to golden ores below,
And in dry desert places tells
Where flow unseen the cool, sweet wells,

So, in the wise Diviner's hand,
Be mine the hazel's grateful part
To feel, beneath a thirsty land,

The living waters thrill and start,
The beating of the rivulet's heart!

Sufficeth me the gift to light
With latest bloom the dark, cold days;
To call some hidden spring to sight
That, in these dry and dusty ways,
Shall sing its pleasant song of praise.

O Love! the hazel–wand may fail,
But thou canst lend the surer spell,
That, passing over Baca's vale,
Repeats the old–time miracle,
And makes the desert–land a well.
1874.

SUNSET ON THE BEARCAMP.

A gold fringe on the purpling hem
Of hills the river runs,
As down its long, green valley falls
The last of summer's suns.

Along its tawny gravel–bed
Broad–flowing, swift, and still,
As if its meadow levels felt
The hurry of the hill,

Noiseless between its banks of green
From curve to curve it slips;
The drowsy maple–shadows rest
Like fingers on its lips.

A waif from Carroll's wildest hills,
Unstoried and unknown;
The ursine legend of its name
Prowls on its banks alone.
Yet flowers as fair its slopes adorn
As ever Yarrow knew,
Or, under rainy Irish skies,
By Spenser's Mulla grew;
And through the gaps of leaning trees
Its mountain cradle shows
The gold against the amethyst,
The green against the rose.

Touched by a light that hath no name,
A glory never sung,
Aloft on sky and mountain wall
Are God's great pictures hung.
How changed the summits vast and old!
No longer granite–browed,
They melt in rosy mist; the rock
Is softer than the cloud;
The valley holds its breath; no leaf
Of all its elms is twirled
The silence of eternity
Seems falling on the world.

The pause before the breaking seals
Of mystery is this;
Yon miracle—play of night and day
Makes dumb its witnesses.
What unseen altar crowns the hills
That reach up stair on stair?
What eyes look through, what white wings fan
These purple veils of air?
What Presence from the heavenly heights
To those of earth stoops down?
Not vainly Hellas dreamed of gods
On Ida's snowy crown!

Slow fades the vision of the sky,
The golden water pales,
And over all the valley—land
A gray—winged vapor sails.
I go the common way of all;
The sunset fires will burn,
The flowers will blow, the river flow,
When I no more return.
No whisper from the mountain pine
Nor lapsing stream shall tell
The stranger, treading where I tread,
Of him who loved them well.

But beauty seen is never lost,
God's colors all are fast;
The glory of this sunset heaven
Into my soul has passed,
A sense of gladness unconfined

To mortal date or clime;
As the soul liveth, it shall live
Beyond the years of time.
Beside the mystic asphodels
Shall bloom the home–born flowers,
And new horizons flush and glow
With sunset hues of ours.

Farewell! these smiling hills must wear
Too soon their wintry frown,
And snow–cold winds from off them shake
The maple's red leaves down.
But I shall see a summer sun
Still setting broad and low;
The mountain slopes shall blush and bloom,
The golden water flow.
A lover's claim is mine on all
I see to have and hold,—
The rose–light of perpetual hills,
And sunsets never cold!
1876

THE SEEKING OF THE WATERFALL.

They left their home of summer ease
Beneath the lowland's sheltering trees,
To seek, by ways unknown to all,
The promise of the waterfall.

Some vague, faint rumor to the vale
Had crept—perchance a hunter's tale—
Of its wild mirth of waters lost
On the dark woods through which it tossed.

Somewhere it laughed and sang; somewhere
Whirled in mad dance its misty hair;
But who had raised its veil, or seen
The rainbow skirts of that Undine?

They sought it where the mountain brook
Its swift way to the valley took;
Along the rugged slope they clomb,
Their guide a thread of sound and foam.

Height after height they slowly won;
The fiery javelins of the sun
Smote the bare ledge; the tangled shade
With rock and vine their steps delayed.

But, through leaf–openings, now and then
They saw the cheerful homes of men,
And the great mountains with their wall
Of misty purple girdling all.

The leaves through which the glad winds blew
Shared. the wild dance the waters knew;
And where the shadows deepest fell
The wood–thrush rang his silver bell.

Fringing the stream, at every turn
Swung low the waving fronds of fern;
From stony cleft and mossy sod
Pale asters sprang, and golden–rod.

And still the water sang the sweet,
Glad song that stirred its gliding feet,
And found in rock and root the keys
Of its beguiling melodies.

Beyond, above, its signals flew
Of tossing foam the birch–trees through;
Now seen, now lost, but baffling still
The weary seekers' slackening will.

Each called to each: "Lo here! Lo there!
Its white scarf flutters in the air!"
They climbed anew; the vision fled,
To beckon higher overhead.

So toiled they up the mountain–slope
With faint and ever fainter hope;
With faint and fainter voice the brook
Still bade them listen, pause, and look.

Meanwhile below the day was done;
Above the tall peaks saw the sun
Sink, beam–shorn, to its misty set
Behind the hills of violet.

"Here ends our quest!" the seekers cried,
"The brook and rumor both have lied!
The phantom of a waterfall
Has led us at its beck and call."

But one, with years grown wiser, said
"So, always baffled, not misled,
We follow where before us runs
The vision of the shining ones.

"Not where they seem their signals fly,
Their voices while we listen die;
We cannot keep, however fleet,
The quick time of their winged feet.

"From youth to age unresting stray
These kindly mockers in our way;
Yet lead they not, the baffling elves,
To something better than themselves?

"Here, though unreached the goal we sought,
Its own reward our toil has brought:
The winding water's sounding rush,
The long note of the hermit thrush,

"The turquoise lakes, the glimpse of pond
And river track, and, vast, beyond
Broad meadows belted round with pines,
The grand uplift of mountain lines!

"What matter though we seek with pain
The garden of the gods in vain,
If lured thereby we climb to greet
Some wayside blossom Eden–sweet?

"To seek is better than to gain,
The fond hope dies as we attain;
Life's fairest things are those which seem,
The best is that of which we dream.

"Then let us trust our waterfall
Still flashes down its rocky wall,
With rainbow crescent curved across
Its sunlit spray from moss to moss.

"And we, forgetful of our pain,
In thought shall seek it oft again;
Shall see this aster–blossomed sod,
This sunshine of the golden–rod,

"And haply gain, through parting boughs,
Grand glimpses of great mountain brows
Cloud–turbaned, and the sharp steel sheen
Of lakes deep set in valleys green.

"So failure wins; the consequence
Of loss becomes its recompense;
And evermore the end shall tell
The unreached ideal guided well.

"Our sweet illusions only die
Fulfilling love's sure prophecy;
And every wish for better things
An undreamed beauty nearer brings.

"For fate is servitor of love;
Desire and hope and longing prove
The secret of immortal youth,
And Nature cheats us into truth.

"O kind allurers, wisely sent,
Beguiling with benign intent,
Still move us, through divine unrest,
To seek the loveliest and the best!

"Go with us when our souls go free,
And, in the clear, white light to be,
Add unto Heaven's beatitude
The old delight of seeking good!"
1878.

THE TRAILING ARBUTUS

I wandered lonely where the pine–trees made
Against the bitter East their barricade,
And, guided by its sweet
Perfume, I found, within a narrow dell,
The trailing spring flower tinted like a shell
Amid dry leaves and mosses at my feet.

From under dead boughs, for whose loss the pines

Moaned ceaseless overhead, the blossoming vines
Lifted their glad surprise,
While yet the bluebird smoothed in leafless trees
His feathers ruffled by the chill sea–breeze,
And snow–drifts lingered under April skies.

As, pausing, o'er the lonely flower I bent,
I thought of lives thus lowly, clogged and pent,
Which yet find room,
Through care and cumber, coldness and decay,
To lend a sweetness to the ungenial day
And make the sad earth happier for their bloom.
1879.

ST. MARTIN'S SUMMER.

This name in some parts of Europe is given to the season we call
Indian Summer, in honor of the good St. Martin. The title of the
poem was suggested by the fact that the day it refers to was the
exact date of that set apart to the Saint, the 11th of November.

Though flowers have perished at the touch
Of Frost, the early comer,
I hail the season loved so much,
The good St. Martin's summer.

O gracious morn, with rose–red dawn,
And thin moon curving o'er it!

91

The old year's darling, latest born,
More loved than all before it!

How flamed the sunrise through the pines!
How stretched the birchen shadows,
Braiding in long, wind—wavered lines
The westward sloping meadows!

The sweet day, opening as a flower
Unfolds its petals tender,
Renews for us at noontide's hour
The summer's tempered splendor.

The birds are hushed; alone the wind,
That through the woodland searches,
The red—oak's lingering leaves can find,
And yellow plumes of larches.

But still the balsam—breathing pine
Invites no thought of sorrow,
No hint of loss from air like wine
The earth's content can borrow.

The summer and the winter here
Midway a truce are holding,
A soft, consenting atmosphere

Their tents of peace enfolding.

The silent woods, the lonely hills,
Rise solemn in their gladness;
The quiet that the valley fills
Is scarcely joy or sadness.

How strange! The autumn yesterday
In winter's grasp seemed dying;
On whirling winds from skies of gray
The early snow was flying.

And now, while over Nature's mood
There steals a soft relenting,
I will not mar the present good,
Forecasting or lamenting.

My autumn time and Nature's hold
A dreamy tryst together,
And, both grown old, about us fold
The golden–tissued weather.

I lean my heart against the day
To feel its bland caressing;
I will not let it pass away
Before it leaves its blessing.

God's angels come not as of old
The Syrian shepherds knew them;
In reddening dawns, in sunset gold,
And warm noon lights I view them.

Nor need there is, in times like this
When heaven to earth draws nearer,
Of wing or song as witnesses
To make their presence clearer.

O stream of life, whose swifter flow
Is of the end forewarning,
Methinks thy sundown afterglow
Seems less of night than morning!

Old cares grow light; aside I lay
The doubts and fears that troubled;
The quiet of the happy day
Within my soul is doubled.

That clouds must veil this fair sunshine
Not less a joy I find it;
Nor less yon warm horizon line
That winter lurks behind it.

The mystery of the untried days
I close my eyes from reading;
His will be done whose darkest ways
To light and life are leading!

Less drear the winter night shall be,
If memory cheer and hearten
Its heavy hours with thoughts of thee,
Sweet summer of St. Martin!
1880.

STORM ON LAKE ASQUAM.

A cloud, like that the old–time Hebrew saw
On Carmel prophesying rain, began
To lift itself o'er wooded Cardigan,
Growing and blackening. Suddenly, a flaw

Of chill wind menaced; then a strong blast beat
Down the long valley's murmuring pines, and woke
The noon–dream of the sleeping lake, and broke
Its smooth steel mirror at the mountains' feet.

Thunderous and vast, a fire–veined darkness swept
Over the rough pine–bearded Asquam range;
A wraith of tempest, wonderful and strange,

From peak to peak the cloudy giant stepped.

One moment, as if challenging the storm,
Chocorua's tall, defiant sentinel
Looked from his watch–tower; then the shadow fell,
And the wild rain–drift blotted out his form.

And over all the still unhidden sun,
Weaving its light through slant–blown veils of rain,
Smiled on the trouble, as hope smiles on pain;
And, when the tumult and the strife were done,

With one foot on the lake and one on land,
Framing within his crescent's tinted streak
A far–off picture of the Melvin peak,
Spent broken clouds the rainbow's angel spanned.
1882.

A SUMMER PILGRIMAGE.

To kneel before some saintly shrine,
To breathe the health of airs divine,
Or bathe where sacred rivers flow,
The cowled and turbaned pilgrims go.
I too, a palmer, take, as they
With staff and scallop–shell, my way
To feel, from burdening cares and ills,

The strong uplifting of the hills.

The years are many since, at first,
For dreamed–of wonders all athirst,
I saw on Winnipesaukee fall
The shadow of the mountain wall.
Ah! where are they who sailed with me
The beautiful island–studded sea?
And am I he whose keen surprise
Flashed out from such unclouded eyes?

Still, when the sun of summer burns,
My longing for the hills returns;
And northward, leaving at my back
The warm vale of the Merrimac,
I go to meet the winds of morn,
Blown down the hill–gaps, mountain–born,
Breathe scent of pines, and satisfy
The hunger of a lowland eye.

Again I see the day decline
Along a ridged horizon line;
Touching the hill–tops, as a nun
Her beaded rosary, sinks the sun.
One lake lies golden, which shall soon
Be silver in the rising moon;
And one, the crimson of the skies
And mountain purple multiplies.

With the untroubled quiet blends
The distance—softened voice of friends;
The girl's light laugh no discord brings
To the low song the pine—tree sings;
And, not unwelcome, comes the hail
Of boyhood from his nearing sail.
The human presence breaks no spell,
And sunset still is miracle!

Calm as the hour, methinks I feel
A sense of worship o'er me steal;
Not that of satyr—charming Pan,
No cult of Nature shaming man,
Not Beauty's self, but that which lives
And shines through all the veils it weaves,—
Soul of the mountain, lake, and wood,
Their witness to the Eternal Good!

And if, by fond illusion, here
The earth to heaven seems drawing near,
And yon outlying range invites
To other and serener heights,
Scarce hid behind its topmost swell,
The shining Mounts Delectable
A dream may hint of truth no less
Than the sharp light of wakefulness.

As through her vale of incense smoke.
Of old the spell—rapt priestess spoke,

More than her heathen oracle,
May not this trance of sunset tell
That Nature's forms of loveliness
Their heavenly archetypes confess,
Fashioned like Israel's ark alone
From patterns in the Mount made known?

A holier beauty overbroods
These fair and faint similitudes;
Yet not unblest is he who sees
Shadows of God's realities,
And knows beyond this masquerade
Of shape and color, light and shade,
And dawn and set, and wax and wane,
Eternal verities remain.

O gems of sapphire, granite set!
O hills that charmed horizons fret
I know how fair your morns can break,
In rosy light on isle and lake;
How over wooded slopes can run
The noonday play of cloud and sun,
And evening droop her oriflamme
Of gold and red in still Asquam.

The summer moons may round again,
And careless feet these hills profane;
These sunsets waste on vacant eyes
The lavish splendor of the skies;
Fashion and folly, misplaced here,

Sigh for their natural atmosphere,
And travelled pride the outlook scorn
Of lesser heights than Matterhorn.

But let me dream that hill and sky
Of unseen beauty prophesy;
And in these tinted lakes behold
The trailing of the raiment fold
Of that which, still eluding gaze,
Allures to upward–tending ways,
Whose footprints make, wherever found,
Our common earth a holy ground.
1883.

SWEET FERN.

The subtle power in perfume found
Nor priest nor sibyl vainly learned;
On Grecian shrine or Aztec mound
No censer idly burned.

That power the old–time worships knew,
The Corybantes' frenzied dance,
The Pythian priestess swooning through
The wonderland of trance.

And Nature holds, in wood and field,

Poems of Nature, Poems Subjective and Reminiscent

Her thousand sunlit censers still;
To spells of flower and shrub we yield
Against or with our will.

I climbed a hill path strange and new
With slow feet, pausing at each turn;
A sudden waft of west wind blew
The breath of the sweet fern.

That fragrance from my vision swept
The alien landscape; in its stead,
Up fairer hills of youth I stepped,
As light of heart as tread.

I saw my boyhood's lakelet shine
Once more through rifts of woodland shade;
I knew my river's winding line
By morning mist betrayed.

With me June's freshness, lapsing brook,
Murmurs of leaf and bee, the call
Of birds, and one in voice and look
In keeping with them all.

A fern beside the way we went
She plucked, and, smiling, held it up,

While from her hand the wild, sweet scent
I drank as from a cup.

O potent witchery of smell!
The dust—dry leaves to life return,
And she who plucked them owns the spell
And lifts her ghostly fern.

Or sense or spirit? Who shall say
What touch the chord of memory thrills?
It passed, and left the August day
Ablaze on lonely hills.

THE WOOD GIANT

From Alton Bay to Sandwich Dome,
From Mad to Saco river,
For patriarchs of the primal wood
We sought with vain endeavor.

And then we said: "The giants old
Are lost beyond retrieval;
This pygmy growth the axe has spared
Is not the wood primeval.

"Look where we will o'er vale and hill,
How idle are our searches
For broad–girthed maples, wide–limbed oaks,
Centennial pines and birches.

"Their tortured limbs the axe and saw
Have changed to beams and trestles;
They rest in walls, they float on seas,
They rot in sunken vessels.

"This shorn and wasted mountain land
Of underbrush and boulder,—
Who thinks to see its full–grown tree
Must live a century older."

At last to us a woodland path,
To open sunset leading,
Revealed the Anakim of pines
Our wildest wish exceeding.

Alone, the level sun before;
Below, the lake's green islands;
Beyond, in misty distance dim,
The rugged Northern Highlands.

Dark Titan on his Sunset Hill
Of time and change defiant
How dwarfed the common woodland seemed,
Before the old–time giant!

What marvel that, in simpler days
Of the world's early childhood,
Men crowned with garlands, gifts, and praise
Such monarchs of the wild–wood?

That Tyrian maids with flower and song
Danced through the hill grove's spaces,
And hoary–bearded Druids found
In woods their holy places?

With somewhat of that Pagan awe
With Christian reverence blending,
We saw our pine–tree's mighty arms
Above our heads extending.

We heard his needles' mystic rune,
Now rising, and now dying,
As erst Dodona's priestess heard
The oak leaves prophesying.

Was it the half–unconscious moan
Of one apart and mateless,
The weariness of unshared power,
The loneliness of greatness?

O dawns and sunsets, lend to him
Your beauty and your wonder!
Blithe sparrow, sing thy summer song
His solemn shadow under!

Play lightly on his slender keys,
O wind of summer, waking
For hills like these the sound of seas
On far–off beaches breaking,

And let the eagle and the crow
Find shelter in his branches,
When winds shake down his winter snow
In silver avalanches.

The brave are braver for their cheer,
The strongest need assurance,
The sigh of longing makes not less
The lesson of endurance.
1885.

A DAY.

**Talk not of sad November, when a day
Of warm, glad sunshine fills the sky of noon,
And a wind, borrowed from some morn of June,
Stirs the brown grasses and the leafless spray.**

On the unfrosted pool the pillared pines
Lay their long shafts of shadow: the small rill,
Singing a pleasant song of summer still,
A line of silver, down the hill–slope shines.

Hushed the bird–voices and the hum of bees,
In the thin grass the crickets pipe no more;
But still the squirrel hoards his winter store,
And drops his nut–shells from the shag–bark trees.

Softly the dark green hemlocks whisper: high
Above, the spires of yellowing larches show,
Where the woodpecker and home–loving crow
And jay and nut–hatch winter's threat defy.

O gracious beauty, ever new and old!
O sights and sounds of nature, doubly dear
When the low sunshine warns the closing year
Of snow–blown fields and waves of Arctic cold!

Close to my heart I fold each lovely thing
The sweet day yields; and, not disconsolate,
With the calm patience of the woods I wait
For leaf and blossom when God gives us Spring!
29th, Eleventh Month, 1886.

POEMS SUBJECTIVE AND REMINISCENT
MEMORIES

A beautiful and happy girl,
With step as light as summer air,
Eyes glad with smiles, and brow of pearl,
Shadowed by many a careless curl
Of unconfined and flowing hair;
A seeming child in everything,
Save thoughtful brow and ripening charms,
As Nature wears the smile of Spring
When sinking into Summer's arms.

A mind rejoicing in the light
Which melted through its graceful bower,
Leaf after leaf, dew-moist and bright,
And stainless in its holy white,

Unfolding like a morning flower
A heart, which, like a fine–toned lute,
With every breath of feeling woke,
And, even when the tongue was mute,
From eye and lip in music spoke.

How thrills once more the lengthening chain
Of memory, at the thought of thee!
Old hopes which long in dust have lain
Old dreams, come thronging back again,
And boyhood lives again in me;
I feel its glow upon my cheek,
Its fulness of the heart is mine,
As when I leaned to hear thee speak,
Or raised my doubtful eye to thine.

I hear again thy low replies,
I feel thy arm within my own,
And timidly again uprise
The fringed lids of hazel eyes,
With soft brown tresses overblown.
Ah! memories of sweet summer eves,
Of moonlit wave and willowy way,
Of stars and flowers, and dewy leaves,
And smiles and tones more dear than they!

Ere this, thy quiet eye hath smiled
My picture of thy youth to see,
When, half a woman, half a child,
Thy very artlessness beguiled,

And folly's self seemed wise in thee;
I too can smile, when o'er that hour
The lights of memory backward stream,
Yet feel the while that manhood's power
Is vainer than my boyhood's dream.

Years have passed on, and left their trace,
Of graver care and deeper thought;
And unto me the calm, cold face
Of manhood, and to thee the grace
Of woman's pensive beauty brought.
More wide, perchance, for blame than praise,
The school—boy's humble name has flown;
Thine, in the green and quiet ways
Of unobtrusive goodness known.

And wider yet in thought and deed
Diverge our pathways, one in youth;
Thine the Genevan's sternest creed,
While answers to my spirit's need
The Derby dalesman's simple truth.
For thee, the priestly rite and prayer,
And holy day, and solemn psalm;
For me, the silent reverence where
My brethren gather, slow and calm.

Yet hath thy spirit left on me
An impress Time has worn not out,
And something of myself in thee,
A shadow from the past, I see,

Lingering, even yet, thy way about;
Not wholly can the heart unlearn
That lesson of its better hours,
Not yet has Time's dull footstep worn
To common dust that path of flowers.

Thus, while at times before our eyes
The shadows melt, and fall apart,
And, smiling through them, round us lies
The warm light of our morning skies,—
The Indian Summer of the heart!
In secret sympathies of mind,
In founts of feeling which retain
Their pure, fresh flow, we yet may find
Our early dreams not wholly vain
1841.

RAPHAEL.

Suggested by the portrait of Raphael, at the age of fifteen.

I shall not soon forget that sight
The glow of Autumn's westering day,
A hazy warmth, a dreamy light,
On Raphael's picture lay.

It was a simple print I saw,

The fair face of a musing boy;
Yet, while I gazed, a sense of awe
Seemed blending with my joy.

A simple print,—the graceful flow
Of boyhood's soft and wavy hair,
And fresh young lip and cheek, and brow
Unmarked and clear, were there.

Yet through its sweet and calm repose
I saw the inward spirit shine;
It was as if before me rose
The white veil of a shrine.

As if, as Gothland's sage has told,
The hidden life, the man within,
Dissevered from its frame and mould,
By mortal eye were seen.

Was it the lifting of that eye,
The waving of that pictured hand?
Loose as a cloud–wreath on the sky,
I saw the walls expand.

The narrow room had vanished,—space,
Broad, luminous, remained alone,

Through which all hues and shapes of grace
And beauty looked or shone.

Around the mighty master came
The marvels which his pencil wrought,
Those miracles of power whose fame
Is wide as human thought.

There drooped thy more than mortal face,
O Mother, beautiful and mild
Enfolding in one dear embrace
Thy Saviour and thy Child!

The rapt brow of the Desert John;
The awful glory of that day
When all the Father's brightness shone
Through manhood's veil of clay.

And, midst gray prophet forms, and wild
Dark visions of the days of old,
How sweetly woman's beauty smiled
Through locks of brown and gold!

There Fornarina's fair young face
Once more upon her lover shone,
Whose model of an angel's grace

He borrowed from her own.

Slow passed that vision from my view,
But not the lesson which it taught;
The soft, calm shadows which it threw
Still rested on my thought:

The truth, that painter, bard, and sage,
Even in Earth's cold and changeful clime,
Plant for their deathless heritage
The fruits and flowers of time.

We shape ourselves the joy or fear
Of which the coming life is made,
And fill our Future's atmosphere
With sunshine or with shade.

The tissue of the Life to be
We weave with colors all our own,
And in the field of Destiny
We reap as we have sown.

Still shall the soul around it call
The shadows which it gathered here,
And, painted on the eternal wall,
The Past shall reappear.

Think ye the notes of holy song
On Milton's tuneful ear have died?
Think ye that Raphael's angel throng
Has vanished from his side?

Oh no!—We live our life again;
Or warmly touched, or coldly dim,
The pictures of the Past remain,—–
Man's works shall follow him!
1842.

EGO.

WRITTEN IN THE ALBUM OF A FRIEND.

On page of thine I cannot trace
The cold and heartless commonplace,
A statue's fixed and marble grace.

For ever as these lines I penned,
Still with the thought of thee will blend
That of some loved and common friend,

Poems of Nature, Poems Subjective and Reminiscent

Who in life's desert track has made
His pilgrim tent with mine, or strayed
Beneath the same remembered shade.

And hence my pen unfettered moves
In freedom which the heart approves,
The negligence which friendship loves.

And wilt thou prize my poor gift less
For simple air and rustic dress,
And sign of haste and carelessness?

Oh, more than specious counterfeit
Of sentiment or studied wit,
A heart like thine should value it.

Yet half I fear my gift will be
Unto thy book, if not to thee,
Of more than doubtful courtesy.

A banished name from Fashion's sphere,
A lay unheard of Beauty's ear,
Forbid, disowned,—what do they here?

Upon my ear not all in vain
Came the sad captive's clanking chain,
The groaning from his bed of pain.

And sadder still, I saw the woe
Which only wounded spirits know
When Pride's strong footsteps o'er them go.

Spurned not alone in walks abroad,
But from the temples of the Lord
Thrust out apart, like things abhorred.

Deep as I felt, and stern and strong,
In words which Prudence smothered long,
My soul spoke out against the wrong;

Not mine alone the task to speak
Of comfort to the poor and weak,
And dry the tear on Sorrow's cheek;

But, mingled in the conflict warm,
To pour the fiery breath of storm
Through the harsh trumpet of Reform;

To brave Opinion's settled frown,
From ermined robe and saintly gown,
While wrestling reverenced Error down.

Founts gushed beside my pilgrim way,
Cool shadows on the greensward lay,
Flowers swung upon the bending spray.

And, broad and bright, on either hand,
Stretched the green slopes of Fairy–land,
With Hope's eternal sunbow spanned;

Whence voices called me like the flow,
Which on the listener's ear will grow,
Of forest streamlets soft and low.

And gentle eyes, which still retain
Their picture on the heart and brain,
Smiled, beckoning from that path of pain.

In vain! nor dream, nor rest, nor pause
Remain for him who round him draws
The battered mail of Freedom's cause.

From youthful hopes, from each green spot
Of young Romance, and gentle Thought,
Where storm and tumult enter not;

From each fair altar, where belong
The offerings Love requires of Song
In homage to her bright—eyed throng;

With soul and strength, with heart and hand,
I turned to Freedom's struggling band,
To the sad Helots of our land.

What marvel then that Fame should turn
Her notes of praise to those of scorn;
Her gifts reclaimed, her smiles withdrawn?

What matters it? a few years more,
Life's surge so restless heretofore
Shall break upon the unknown shore!

In that far land shall disappear
The shadows which we follow here,
The mist—wreaths of our atmosphere!

Before no work of mortal hand,
Of human will or strength expand
The pearl gates of the Better Land;

Alone in that great love which gave
Life to the sleeper of the grave,
Resteth the power to seek and save.

Yet, if the spirit gazing through
The vista of the past can view
One deed to Heaven and virtue true;

If through the wreck of wasted powers,
Of garlands wreathed from Folly's bowers,
Of idle aims and misspent hours,

The eye can note one sacred spot
By Pride and Self profaned not,
A green place in the waste of thought,

Where deed or word hath rendered less
The sum of human wretchedness,
And Gratitude looks forth to bless;

Poems of Nature, Poems Subjective and Reminiscent

The simple burst of tenderest feeling
From sad hearts worn by evil–dealing,
For blessing on the hand of healing;

Better than Glory's pomp will be
That green and blessed spot to me,
A palm–shade in Eternity!

Something of Time which may invite
The purified and spiritual sight
To rest on with a calm delight.

And when the summer winds shall sweep
With their light wings my place of sleep,
And mosses round my headstone creep;

If still, as Freedom's rallying sign,
Upon the young heart's altars shine
The very fires they caught from mine;

If words my lips once uttered still,
In the calm faith and steadfast will
Of other hearts, their work fulfil;

120

Perchance with joy the soul may learn
These tokens, and its eye discern
The fires which on those altars burn;

A marvellous joy that even then,
The spirit hath its life again,
In the strong hearts of mortal men.

Take, lady, then, the gift I bring,
No gay and graceful offering,
No flower—smile of the laughing spring.

Midst the green buds of Youth's fresh May,
With Fancy's leaf—enwoven bay,
My sad and sombre gift I lay.

And if it deepens in thy mind
A sense of suffering human—kind,—
The outcast and the spirit—blind;

Oppressed and spoiled on every side,
By Prejudice, and Scorn, and Pride,
Life's common courtesies denied;

Sad mothers mourning o'er their trust,
Children by want and misery nursed,
Tasting life's bitter cup at first;

If to their strong appeals which come
From fireless hearth, and crowded room,
And the close alley's noisome gloom,—

Though dark the hands upraised to thee
In mute beseeching agony,
Thou lend'st thy woman's sympathy;

Not vainly on thy gentle shrine,
Where Love, and Mirth, and Friendship twine
Their varied gifts, I offer mine.
1843.

THE PUMPKIN.

Oh, greenly and fair in the lands of the sun,
The vines of the gourd and the rich melon run,
And the rock and the tree and the cottage enfold,
With broad leaves all greenness and blossoms all gold,
Like that which o'er Nineveh's prophet once grew,
While he waited to know that his warning was true,
And longed for the storm—cloud, and listened in vain

For the rush of the whirlwind and red fire–rain.

On the banks of the Xenil the dark Spanish maiden
Comes up with the fruit of the tangled vine laden;
And the Creole of Cuba laughs out to behold
Through orange–leaves shining the broad spheres of gold;
Yet with dearer delight from his home in the North,
On the fields of his harvest the Yankee looks forth,
Where crook–necks are coiling and yellow fruit shines,
And the sun of September melts down on his vines.

Ah! on Thanksgiving day, when from East and from West,
From North and from South come the pilgrim and guest,
When the gray–haired New–Englander sees round his board
The old broken links of affection restored,
When the care–wearied man seeks his mother once more,
And the worn matron smiles where the girl smiled before,
What moistens the lip and what brightens the eye?
What calls back the past, like the rich Pumpkin pie?

Oh, fruit loved of boyhood! the old days recalling,
When wood–grapes were purpling and brown nuts were falling!
When wild, ugly faces we carved in its skin,
Glaring out through the dark with a candle within!
When we laughed round the corn–heap, with hearts all in tune,
Our chair a broad pumpkin,—our lantern the moon,
Telling tales of the fairy who travelled like steam,
In a pumpkin–shell coach, with two rats for her team
Then thanks for thy present! none sweeter or better
E'er smoked from an oven or circled a platter!

Fairer hands never wrought at a pastry more fine,
Brighter eyes never watched o'er its baking, than thine!
And the prayer, which my mouth is too full to express,
Swells my heart that thy shadow may never be less,
That the days of thy lot may be lengthened below,
And the fame of thy worth like a pumpkin−vine grow,
And thy life be as sweet, and its last sunset sky
Golden−tinted and fair as thy own Pumpkin pie!
1844.

FORGIVENESS.

My heart was heavy, for its trust had been
Abused, its kindness answered with foul wrong;
So, turning gloomily from my fellow−men,
One summer Sabbath day I strolled among
The green mounds of the village burial−place;
Where, pondering how all human love and hate
Find one sad level; and how, soon or late,
Wronged and wrongdoer, each with meekened face,
And cold hands folded over a still heart,
Pass the green threshold of our common grave,
Whither all footsteps tend, whence none depart,
Awed for myself, and pitying my race,
Our common sorrow, like a nighty wave,
Swept all my pride away, and trembling I forgave!
1846.

TO MY SISTER,

WITH A COPY OF "THE SUPERNATURALISM OF NEW ENGLAND."

Poems of Nature, Poems Subjective and Reminiscent

The work referred to was a series of papers under this title,
contributed to the Democratic Review and afterward collected into a
volume, in which I noted some of the superstitions and folklore
prevalent in New England. The volume has not been kept in print,
but most of its contents are distributed in my Literary Recreations
and Miscellanies.

Dear Sister! while the wise and sage
Turn coldly from my playful page,
And count it strange that ripened age
Should stoop to boyhood's folly;
I know that thou wilt judge aright
Of all which makes the heart more light,
Or lends one star–gleam to the night
Of clouded Melancholy.

Away with weary cares and themes!
Swing wide the moonlit gate of dreams!
Leave free once more the land which teems
With wonders and romances
Where thou, with clear discerning eyes,
Shalt rightly read the truth which lies
Beneath the quaintly masking guise
Of wild and wizard fancies.

Lo! once again our feet we set
On still green wood–paths, twilight wet,
By lonely brooks, whose waters fret
The roots of spectral beeches;

Again the hearth–fire glimmers o'er
Home's whitewashed wall and painted floor,
And young eyes widening to the lore
Of faery–folks and witches.

Dear heart! the legend is not vain
Which lights that holy hearth again,
And calling back from care and pain,
And death's funereal sadness,
Draws round its old familiar blaze
The clustering groups of happier days,
And lends to sober manhood's gaze
A glimpse of childish gladness.

And, knowing how my life hath been
A weary work of tongue and pen,
A long, harsh strife with strong–willed men,
Thou wilt not chide my turning
To con, at times, an idle rhyme,
To pluck a flower from childhood's clime,
Or listen, at Life's noonday chime,
For the sweet bells of Morning!
1847.

MY THANKS,

ACCOMPANYING MANUSCRIPTS PRESENTED TO A FRIEND.

'T is said that in the Holy Land
The angels of the place have blessed
The pilgrim's bed of desert sand,
Like Jacob's stone of rest.

That down the hush of Syrian skies
Some sweet–voiced saint at twilight sings
The song whose holy symphonies
Are beat by unseen wings;

Till starting from his sandy bed,
The wayworn wanderer looks to see
The halo of an angel's head
Shine through the tamarisk–tree.

So through the shadows of my way
Thy smile hath fallen soft and clear,
So at the weary close of day
Hath seemed thy voice of cheer.

That pilgrim pressing to his goal
May pause not for the vision's sake,
Yet all fair things within his soul
The thought of it shall wake:

The graceful palm–tree by the well,
Seen on the far horizon's rim;
The dark eyes of the fleet gazelle,
Bent timidly on him;

Each pictured saint, whose golden hair
Streams sunlike through the convent's gloom;
Pale shrines of martyrs young and fair,
And loving Mary's tomb;

And thus each tint or shade which falls,
From sunset cloud or waving tree,
Along my pilgrim path, recalls
The pleasant thought of thee.

Of one in sun and shade the same,
In weal and woe my steady friend,
Whatever by that holy name
The angels comprehend.

Not blind to faults and follies, thou
Hast never failed the good to see,
Nor judged by one unseemly bough
The upward–struggling tree.

Poems of Nature, Poems Subjective and Reminiscent

These light leaves at thy feet I lay,—
Poor common thoughts on common things,
Which time is shaking, day by day,
Like feathers from his wings;

Chance shootings from a frail life–tree,
To nurturing care but little known,
Their good was partly learned of thee,
Their folly is my own.

That tree still clasps the kindly mould,
Its leaves still drink the twilight dew,
And weaving its pale green with gold,
Still shines the sunlight through.

There still the morning zephyrs play,
And there at times the spring bird sings,
And mossy trunk and fading spray
Are flowered with glossy wings.

Yet, even in genial sun and rain,
Root, branch, and leaflet fail and fade;
The wanderer on its lonely plain
Erelong shall miss its shade.

O friend beloved, whose curious skill
Keeps bright the last year's leaves and flowers,
With warm, glad, summer thoughts to fill
The cold, dark, winter hours

Pressed on thy heart, the leaves I bring
May well defy the wintry cold,
Until, in Heaven's eternal spring,
Life's fairer ones unfold.
1847.

REMEMBRANCE

WITH COPIES OF THE AUTHOR'S WRITINGS.

Friend of mine! whose lot was cast
With me in the distant past;
Where, like shadows flitting fast,

Fact and fancy, thought and theme,
Word and work, begin to seem
Like a half—remembered dream!

Touched by change have all things been,

Yet I think of thee as when
We had speech of lip and pen.

For the calm thy kindness lent
To a path of discontent,
Rough with trial and dissent;

Gentle words where such were few,
Softening blame where blame was true,
Praising where small praise was due;

For a waking dream made good,
For an ideal understood,
For thy Christian womanhood;

For thy marvellous gift to cull
From our common life and dull
Whatsoe'er is beautiful;

Thoughts and fancies, Hybla's bees
Dropping sweetness; true heart's—ease
Of congenial sympathies;—

Still for these I own my debt;

Memory, with her eyelids wet,
Fain would thank thee even yet!

And as one who scatters flowers
Where the Queen of May's sweet hours
Sits, o'ertwined with blossomed bowers,

In superfluous zeal bestowing
Gifts where gifts are overflowing,
So I pay the debt I'm owing.

To thy full thoughts, gay or sad,
Sunny—hued or sober clad,
Something of my own I add;

Well assured that thou wilt take
Even the offering which I make
Kindly for the giver's sake.
1851.

MY NAMESAKE.

Addressed to Francis Greenleaf Allison of Burlington, New Jersey.

You scarcely need my tardy thanks,
Who, self—rewarded, nurse and tend—
A green leaf on your own Green Banks—
The memory of your friend.

For me, no wreath, bloom—woven, hides
The sobered brow and lessening hair
For aught I know, the myrtled sides
Of Helicon are bare.

Their scallop—shells so many bring
The fabled founts of song to try,
They've drained, for aught I know, the spring
Of Aganippe dry.

Ah well!—The wreath the Muses braid
Proves often Folly's cap and bell;
Methinks, my ample beaver's shade
May serve my turn as well.

Let Love's and Friendship's tender debt
Be paid by those I love in life.
Why should the unborn critic whet
For me his scalping—knife?

Why should the stranger peer and pry
One's vacant house of life about,
And drag for curious ear and eye
His faults and follies out?—

Why stuff, for fools to gaze upon,
With chaff of words, the garb he wore,
As corn—husks when the ear is gone
Are rustled all the more?

Let kindly Silence close again,
The picture vanish from the eye,
And on the dim and misty main
Let the small ripple die.

Yet not the less I own your claim
To grateful thanks, dear friends of mine.
Hang, if it please you so, my name
Upon your household line.

Let Fame from brazen lips blow wide
Her chosen names, I envy none
A mother's love, a father's pride,
Shall keep alive my own!

Still shall that name as now recall
The young leaf wet with morning dew,
The glory where the sunbeams fall
The breezy woodlands through.

That name shall be a household word,
A spell to waken smile or sigh;
In many an evening prayer be heard
And cradle lullaby.

And thou, dear child, in riper days
When asked the reason of thy name,
Shalt answer: One 't were vain to praise
Or censure bore the same.

"Some blamed him, some believed him good,
The truth lay doubtless 'twixt the two;
He reconciled as best he could
Old faith and fancies new.

"In him the grave and playful mixed,
And wisdom held with folly truce,
And Nature compromised betwixt
Good fellow and recluse.

"He loved his friends, forgave his foes;
And, if his words were harsh at times,
He spared his fellow—men,—his blows
Fell only on their crimes.

"He loved the good and wise, but found
His human heart to all akin
Who met him on the common ground
Of suffering and of sin.

"Whate'er his neighbors might endure
Of pain or grief his own became;
For all the ills he could not cure
He held himself to blame.

"His good was mainly an intent,
His evil not of forethought done;
The work he wrought was rarely meant
Or finished as begun.

"Ill served his tides of feeling strong
To turn the common mills of use;
And, over restless wings of song,
His birthright garb hung loose!

"His eye was beauty's powerless slave,
And his the ear which discord pains;
Few guessed beneath his aspect grave
What passions strove in chains.

"He had his share of care and pain,
No holiday was life to him;
Still in the heirloom cup we drain
The bitter drop will swim.

"Yet Heaven was kind, and here a bird
And there a flower beguiled his way;
And, cool, in summer noons, he heard
The fountains plash and play.

"On all his sad or restless moods
The patient peace of Nature stole;
The quiet of the fields and woods
Sank deep into his soul.

"He worshipped as his fathers did,
And kept the faith of childish days,
And, howsoe'er he strayed or slid,
He loved the good old ways.

"The simple tastes, the kindly traits,
The tranquil air, and gentle speech,
The silence of the soul that waits
For more than man to teach.

"The cant of party, school, and sect,
Provoked at times his honest scorn,
And Folly, in its gray respect,
He tossed on satire's horn.

"But still his heart was full of awe
And reverence for all sacred things;
And, brooding over form and law,'
He saw the Spirit's wings!

"Life's mystery wrapt him like a cloud;
He heard far voices mock his own,
The sweep of wings unseen, the loud,
Long roll of waves unknown.

"The arrows of his straining sight
Fell quenched in darkness; priest and sage,
Like lost guides calling left and right,
Perplexed his doubtful age.

"Like childhood, listening for the sound
Of its dropped pebbles in the well,
All vainly down the dark profound
His brief–lined plummet fell.

"So, scattering flowers with pious pains
On old beliefs, of later creeds,
Which claimed a place in Truth's domains,
He asked the title–deeds.

"He saw the old–time's groves and shrines
In the long distance fair and dim;
And heard, like sound of far–off pines,
The century–mellowed hymn!

"He dared not mock the Dervish whirl,
The Brahmin's rite, the Lama's spell;
God knew the heart; Devotion's pearl
Might sanctify the shell.

"While others trod the altar stairs
He faltered like the publican;
And, while they praised as saints, his prayers
Were those of sinful man.

"For, awed by Sinai's Mount of Law,
The trembling faith alone sufficed,
That, through its cloud and flame, he saw
The sweet, sad face of Christ!

"And listening, with his forehead bowed,
Heard the Divine compassion fill
The pauses of the trump and cloud
With whispers small and still.

"The words he spake, the thoughts he penned,
Are mortal as his hand and brain,
But, if they served the Master's end,
He has not lived in vain!"

Heaven make thee better than thy name,
Child of my friends!—For thee I crave
What riches never bought, nor fame
To mortal longing gave.

I pray the prayer of Plato old:
God make thee beautiful within,
And let thine eyes the good behold
In everything save sin!

Imagination held in check
To serve, not rule, thy poised mind;
Thy Reason, at the frown or beck
Of Conscience, loose or bind.

No dreamer thou, but real all,—
Strong manhood crowning vigorous youth;
Life made by duty epical
And rhythmic with the truth.

So shall that life the fruitage yield
Which trees of healing only give,
And green–leafed in the Eternal field
Of God, forever live!
1853.

A MEMORY

Here, while the loom of Winter weaves
The shroud of flowers and fountains,
I think of thee and summer eves
Among the Northern mountains.

When thunder tolled the twilight's close,
And winds the lake were rude on,
And thou wert singing, *Ca' the Yowes*,

The bonny yowes of Cluden!

When, close and closer, hushing breath,
Our circle narrowed round thee,
And smiles and tears made up the wreath
Wherewith our silence crowned thee;

And, strangers all, we felt the ties
Of sisters and of brothers;
Ah! whose of all those kindly eyes
Now smile upon another's?

The sport of Time, who still apart
The waifs of life is flinging;
Oh, nevermore shall heart to heart
Draw nearer for that singing!

Yet when the panes are frosty–starred,
And twilight's fire is gleaming,
I hear the songs of Scotland's bard
Sound softly through my dreaming!

A song that lends to winter snows
The glow of summer weather,—
Again I hear thee ca' the yowes
To Cluden's hills of heather

1854.

MY DREAM.

In my dream, methought I trod,
Yesternight, a mountain road;
Narrow as Al Sirat's span,
High as eagle's flight, it ran.

Overhead, a roof of cloud
With its weight of thunder bowed;
Underneath, to left and right,
Blankness and abysmal night.

Here and there a wild–flower blushed,
Now and then a bird–song gushed;
Now and then, through rifts of shade,
Stars shone out, and sunbeams played.

But the goodly company,
Walking in that path with me,
One by one the brink o'erslid,
One by one the darkness hid.

Some with wailing and lament,

Some with cheerful courage went;
But, of all who smiled or mourned,
Never one to us returned.

Anxiously, with eye and ear,
Questioning that shadow drear,
Never hand in token stirred,
Never answering voice I heard!

Steeper, darker!—lo! I felt
From my feet the pathway melt.
Swallowed by the black despair,
And the hungry jaws of air,

Past the stony—throated caves,
Strangled by the wash of waves,
Past the splintered crags, I sank
On a green and flowery bank,—

Soft as fall of thistle—down,
Lightly as a cloud is blown,
Soothingly as childhood pressed
To the bosom of its rest.

Of the sharp—horned rocks instead,
Green the grassy meadows spread,

Bright with waters singing by
Trees that propped a golden sky.

Painless, trustful, sorrow—free,
Old lost faces welcomed me,
With whose sweetness of content
Still expectant hope was blent.

Waking while the dawning gray
Slowly brightened into day,
Pondering that vision fled,
Thus unto myself I said:—

"Steep and hung with clouds of strife
Is our narrow path of life;
And our death the dreaded fall
Through the dark, awaiting all.

"So, with painful steps we climb
Up the dizzy ways of time,
Ever in the shadow shed
By the forecast of our dread.

"Dread of mystery solved alone,
Of the untried and unknown;
Yet the end thereof may seem

Like the falling of my dream.

"And this heart–consuming care,
All our fears of here or there,
Change and absence, loss and death,
Prove but simple lack of faith."

Thou, O Most Compassionate!
Who didst stoop to our estate,
Drinking of the cup we drain,
Treading in our path of pain,—

Through the doubt and mystery,
Grant to us thy steps to see,
And the grace to draw from thence
Larger hope and confidence.

Show thy vacant tomb, and let,
As of old, the angels sit,
Whispering, by its open door
"Fear not! He hath gone before!"
1855.

THE BAREFOOT BOY.

Poems of Nature, Poems Subjective and Reminiscent

Blessings on thee, little man,
Barefoot boy, with cheek of tan
With thy turned–up pantaloons,
And thy merry whistled tunes;
With thy red lip, redder still
Kissed by strawberries on the hill;
With the sunshine on thy face,
Through thy torn brim's jaunty grace;
From my heart I give thee joy,—
I was once a barefoot boy!

Prince thou art,—the grown–up man
Only is republican.
Let the million–dollared ride!
Barefoot, trudging at his side,
Thou hast more than he can buy
In the reach of ear and eye,—
Outward sunshine, inward joy
Blessings on thee, barefoot boy!

Oh for boyhood's painless play,
Sleep that wakes in laughing day,
Health that mocks the doctor's rules,
Knowledge never learned of schools,
Of the wild bee's morning chase,
Of the wild–flower's time and place,
Flight of fowl and habitude
Of the tenants of the wood;
How the tortoise bears his shell,
How the woodchuck digs his cell,
And the ground–mole sinks his well;

How the robin feeds her young,
How the oriole's nest is hung;
Where the whitest lilies blow,
Where the freshest berries grow,
Where the ground–nut trails its vine,
Where the wood–grape's clusters shine;
Of the black wasp's cunning way,
Mason of his walls of clay,
And the architectural plans
Of gray hornet artisans!
For, eschewing books and tasks,
Nature answers all he asks,
Hand in hand with her he walks,
Face to face with her he talks,
Part and parcel of her joy,—
Blessings on the barefoot boy!

Oh for boyhood's time of June,
Crowding years in one brief moon,
When all things I heard or saw,
Me, their master, waited for.
I was rich in flowers and trees,
Humming–birds and honey–bees;
For my sport the squirrel played,
Plied the snouted mole his spade;
For my taste the blackberry cone
Purpled over hedge and stone;
Laughed the brook for my delight
Through the day and through the night,
Whispering at the garden wall,
Talked with me from fall to fall;
Mine the sand–rimmed pickerel pond,
Mine the walnut slopes beyond,
Mine, on bending orchard trees,

Apples of Hesperides!
Still as my horizon grew,
Larger grew my riches too;
All the world I saw or knew
Seemed a complex Chinese toy,
Fashioned for a barefoot boy!

Oh for festal dainties spread,
Like my bowl of milk and bread;
Pewter spoon and bowl of wood,
On the door–stone, gray and rude!
O'er me, like a regal tent,
Cloudy–ribbed, the sunset bent,
Purple–curtained, fringed with gold,
Looped in many a wind–swung fold;
While for music came the play
Of the pied frogs' orchestra;
And, to light the noisy choir,
Lit the fly his lamp of fire.
I was monarch: pomp and joy
Waited on the barefoot boy!

Cheerily, then, my little man,
Live and laugh, as boyhood can
Though the flinty slopes be hard,
Stubble–speared the new–mown sward,
Every morn shall lead thee through
Fresh baptisms of the dew;
Every evening from thy feet
Shall the cool wind kiss the heat
All too soon these feet must hide
In the prison cells of pride,

Lose the freedom of the sod,
Like a colt's for work be shod,
Made to tread the mills of toil,
Up and down in ceaseless moil
Happy if their track be found
Never on forbidden ground;
Happy if they sink not in
Quick and treacherous sands of sin.
Ah! that thou couldst know thy joy,
Ere it passes, barefoot boy!
1855.

MY PSALM.

I mourn no more my vanished years
Beneath a tender rain,
An April rain of smiles and tears,
My heart is young again.

The west–winds blow, and, singing low,
I hear the glad streams run;
The windows of my soul I throw
Wide open to the sun.

No longer forward nor behind
I look in hope or fear;
But, grateful, take the good I find,

Poems of Nature, Poems Subjective and Reminiscent

The best of now and here.

I plough no more a desert land,
To harvest weed and tare;
The manna dropping from God's hand
Rebukes my painful care.

I break my pilgrim staff, I lay
Aside the toiling oar;
The angel sought so far away
I welcome at my door.

The airs of spring may never play
Among the ripening corn,
Nor freshness of the flowers of May
Blow through the autumn morn.

Yet shall the blue–eyed gentian look
Through fringed lids to heaven,
And the pale aster in the brook
Shall see its image given;—

The woods shall wear their robes of praise,
The south–wind softly sigh,
And sweet, calm days in golden haze
Melt down the amber sky.

Not less shall manly deed and word
Rebuke an age of wrong;
The graven flowers that wreathe the sword
Make not the blade less strong.

But smiting hands shall learn to heal,—
To build as to destroy;
Nor less my heart for others feel
That I the more enjoy.

All as God wills, who wisely heeds
To give or to withhold,
And knoweth more of all my needs
Than all my prayers have told.

Enough that blessings undeserved
Have marked my erring track;
That wheresoe'er my feet have swerved,
His chastening turned me back;

That more and more a Providence
Of love is understood,
Making the springs of time and sense
Sweet with eternal good;—

That death seems but a covered way
Which opens into light,
Wherein no blinded child can stray
Beyond the Father's sight;

That care and trial seem at last,
Through Memory's sunset air,
Like mountain–ranges overpast,
In purple distance fair;

That all the jarring notes of life
Seem blending in a psalm,
And all the angles of its strife
Slow rounding into calm.

And so the shadows fall apart,
And so the west–winds play;
And all the windows of my heart
I open to the day.
1859.

THE WAITING.

I wait and watch: before my eyes
Methinks the night grows thin and gray;
I wait and watch the eastern skies

To see the golden spears uprise
Beneath the oriflamme of day!

Like one whose limbs are bound in trance
I hear the day–sounds swell and grow,
And see across the twilight glance,
Troop after troop, in swift advance,
The shining ones with plumes of snow!

I know the errand of their feet,
I know what mighty work is theirs;
I can but lift up hands unmeet,
The threshing–floors of God to beat,
And speed them with unworthy prayers.

I will not dream in vain despair
The steps of progress wait for me
The puny leverage of a hair
The planet's impulse well may spare,
A drop of dew the tided sea.

The loss, if loss there be, is mine,
And yet not mine if understood;
For one shall grasp and one resign,
One drink life's rue, and one its wine,
And God shall make the balance good.

Oh power to do! Oh baffled will!
Oh prayer and action! ye are one.
Who may not strive, may yet fulfil
The harder task of standing still,
And good but wished with God is done!
1862.

SNOW-BOUND.

A WINTER IDYL.

TO THE MEMORY

OF

THE HOUSEHOLD IT DESCRIBES,

THIS POEM IS DEDICATED BY THE AUTHOR.

The inmates of the family at the Whittier homestead who are
referred to in the poem were my father, mother, my brother and two
sisters, and my uncle and aunt both unmarried. In addition, there
was the district school-master who boarded with us. The "not
unfeared, half-welcome guest" was Harriet Livermore, daughter of
Judge Livermore, of New Hampshire, a young woman of fine natural
ability, enthusiastic, eccentric, with slight control over her
violent temper, which sometimes made her religious profession
doubtful. She was equally ready to exhort in school-house

155

prayer–meetings and dance in a Washington ball–room, while her father was a member of Congress. She early embraced the doctrine of the Second Advent, and felt it her duty to proclaim the Lord's speedy coming. With this message she crossed the Atlantic and spent the greater part of a long life in travelling over Europe and Asia. She lived some time with Lady Hester Stanhope, a woman as fantastic and mentally strained as herself, on the slope of Mt. Lebanon, but finally quarrelled with her in regard to two white horses with red marks on their backs which suggested the idea of saddles, on which her titled hostess expected to ride into Jerusalem with the Lord. A friend of mine found her, when quite an old woman, wandering in Syria with a tribe of Arabs, who with the Oriental notion that madness is inspiration, accepted her as their prophetess and leader. At the time referred to in Snow–Bound she was boarding at the Rocks Village about two miles from us.

In my boyhood, in our lonely farm–house, we had scanty sources of information; few books and only a small weekly newspaper. Our only annual was the Almanac. Under such circumstances story–telling was a necessary resource in the long winter evenings. My father when a young man had traversed the wilderness to Canada, and could tell us of his adventures with Indians and wild beasts, and of his sojourn in the French villages. My uncle was ready with his record of hunting and fishing and, it must be confessed, with stories which he at least half believed, of witchcraft and apparitions. My mother, who was born in the Indian–haunted region of Somersworth, New Hampshire, between Dover and Portsmouth, told us of the inroads of the savages, and the narrow escape of her ancestors. She described strange people who lived on the Piscataqua and Cocheco, among whom was Bantam the sorcerer. I have in my possession the wizard's "conjuring book," which he solemnly opened when consulted. It is a copy of Cornelius Agrippa's Magic printed in 1651, dedicated to Dr. Robert Child, who, like Michael Scott, had learned "the art of glammorie In Padua beyond the sea," and who is famous in the annals of Massachusetts, where he was at one time a resident, as the first man who dared petition the General Court for liberty of conscience. The full title of the book is Three Books of Occult Philosophy, by Henry Cornelius Agrippa, Knight, Doctor of both Laws, Counsellor to Caesar's Sacred Majesty and Judge of the Prerogative Court.

"As the Spirits of Darkness be stronger in the dark, so Good
Spirits, which be Angels of Light, are augmented not only by the
Divine light of the Sun, but also by our common Wood Fire: and as
the Celestial Fire drives away dark spirits, so also this our Fire
of Wood doth the same."—Cor. AGRIPPA, Occult Philosophy, Book I.
ch. v.

"Announced by all the trumpets of the sky,
Arrives the snow, and, driving o'er the fields,
Seems nowhere to alight: the whited air
Hides hills and woods, the rivet and the heaven,
And veils the farm–house at the garden's end.
The sled and traveller stopped, the courier's feet
Delayed, all friends shut out, the housemates sit
Around the radiant fireplace, enclosed
In a tumultuous privacy of storm."
            Emerson. The Snow Storm.

The sun that brief December day
Rose cheerless over hills of gray,
And, darkly circled, gave at noon
A sadder light than waning moon.
Slow tracing down the thickening sky
Its mute and ominous prophecy,
A portent seeming less than threat,

It sank from sight before it set.
A chill no coat, however stout,
Of homespun stuff could quite, shut out,
A hard, dull bitterness of cold,
That checked, mid—vein, the circling race
Of life—blood in the sharpened face,
The coming of the snow—storm told.
The wind blew east; we heard the roar
Of Ocean on his wintry shore,
And felt the strong pulse throbbing there
Beat with low rhythm our inland air.

Meanwhile we did our nightly chores,—
Brought in the wood from out of doors,
Littered the stalls, and from the mows
Raked down the herd's—grass for the cows
Heard the horse whinnying for his corn;
And, sharply clashing horn on horn,
Impatient down the stanchion rows
The cattle shake their walnut bows;
While, peering from his early perch
Upon the scaffold's pole of birch,
The cock his crested helmet bent
And down his querulous challenge sent.

Unwarmed by any sunset light
The gray day darkened into night,
A night made hoary with the swarm,
And whirl—dance of the blinding storm,
As zigzag, wavering to and fro,
Crossed and recrossed the winged snow
And ere the early bedtime came

The white drift piled the window—frame,
And through the glass the clothes—line posts
Looked in like tall and sheeted ghosts.

So all night long the storm roared on
The morning broke without a sun;
In tiny spherule traced with lines
Of Nature's geometric signs,
In starry flake, and pellicle,
All day the hoary meteor fell;
And, when the second morning shone,
We looked upon a world unknown,
On nothing we could call our own.
Around the glistening wonder bent
The blue walls of the firmament,
No cloud above, no earth below,—
A universe of sky and snow
The old familiar sights of ours
Took marvellous shapes; strange domes and towers
Rose up where sty or corn—crib stood,
Or garden—wall, or belt of wood;
A smooth white mound the brush—pile showed,
A fenceless drift what once was road;
The bridle—post an old man sat
With loose—flung coat and high cocked hat;
The well—curb had a Chinese roof;
And even the long sweep, high aloof,
In its slant splendor, seemed to tell
Of Pisa's leaning miracle.

A prompt, decisive man, no breath
Our father wasted: "Boys, a path!"

Well pleased, (for when did farmer boy
Count such a summons less than joy?)
Our buskins on our feet we drew;
With mittened hands, and caps drawn low,
To guard our necks and ears from snow,
We cut the solid whiteness through.
And, where the drift was deepest, made
A tunnel walled and overlaid
With dazzling crystal: we had read
Of rare Aladdin's wondrous cave,
And to our own his name we gave,
With many a wish the luck were ours
To test his lamp's supernal powers.
We reached the barn with merry din,
And roused the prisoned brutes within.
The old horse thrust his long head out,
And grave with wonder gazed about;
The cock his lusty greeting said,
And forth his speckled harem led;
The oxen lashed their tails, and hooked,
And mild reproach of hunger looked;
The horned patriarch of the sheep,
Like Egypt's Amun roused from sleep,
Shook his sage head with gesture mute,
And emphasized with stamp of foot.

All day the gusty north–wind bore
The loosening drift its breath before;
Low circling round its southern zone,
The sun through dazzling snow–mist shone.
No church–bell lent its Christian tone
To the savage air, no social smoke
Curled over woods of snow–hung oak.
A solitude made more intense

By dreary–voiced elements,
The shrieking of the mindless wind,
The moaning tree–boughs swaying blind,
And on the glass the unmeaning beat
Of ghostly finger–tips of sleet.
Beyond the circle of our hearth
No welcome sound of toil or mirth
Unbound the spell, and testified
Of human life and thought outside.
We minded that the sharpest ear
The buried brooklet could not hear,
The music of whose liquid lip
Had been to us companionship,
And, in our lonely life, had grown
To have an almost human tone.

As night drew on, and, from the crest
Of wooded knolls that ridged the west,
The sun, a snow–blown traveller, sank
From sight beneath the smothering bank,
We piled, with care, our nightly stack
Of wood against the chimney–back,—
The oaken log, green, huge, and thick,
And on its top the stout back–stick;
The knotty forestick laid apart,
And filled between with curious art
The ragged brush; then, hovering near,
We watched the first red blaze appear,
Heard the sharp crackle, caught the gleam
On whitewashed wall and sagging beam,
Until the old, rude–furnished room
Burst, flower–like, into rosy bloom;
While radiant with a mimic flame
Outside the sparkling drift became,

And through the bare—boughed lilac—tree
Our own warm hearth seemed blazing free.
The crane and pendent trammels showed,
The Turks' heads on the andirons glowed;
While childish fancy, prompt to tell
The meaning of the miracle,
Whispered the old rhyme: *"Under the tree,*
When fire outdoors burns merrily,
There the witches are making tea."

The moon above the eastern wood
Shone at its full; the hill—range stood
Transfigured in the silver flood,
Its blown snows flashing cold and keen,
Dead white, save where some sharp ravine
Took shadow, or the sombre green
Of hemlocks turned to pitchy black
Against the whiteness at their back.
For such a world and such a night
Most fitting that unwarming light,
Which only seemed where'er it fell
To make the coldness visible.

Shut in from all the world without,
We sat the clean—winged hearth about,
Content to let the north—wind roar
In baffled rage at pane and door,
While the red logs before us beat
The frost—line back with tropic heat;
And ever, when a louder blast
Shook beam and rafter as it passed,
The merrier up its roaring draught

The great throat of the chimney laughed;
The house–dog on his paws outspread
Laid to the fire his drowsy head,
The cat's dark silhouette on the wall
A couchant tiger's seemed to fall;
And, for the winter fireside meet,
Between the andirons' straddling feet,
The mug of cider simmered slow,
The apples sputtered in a row,
And, close at hand, the basket stood
With nuts from brown October's wood.

What matter how the night behaved?
What matter how the north–wind raved?
Blow high, blow low, not all its snow
Could quench our hearth–fire's ruddy glow.
O Time and Change!—with hair as gray
As was my sire's that winter day,
How strange it seems, with so much gone
Of life and love, to still live on!
Ah, brother! only I and thou
Are left of all that circle now,—
The dear home faces whereupon
That fitful firelight paled and shone.
Henceforward, listen as we will,
The voices of that hearth are still;
Look where we may, the wide earth o'er
Those lighted faces smile no more.
We tread the paths their feet have worn,
We sit beneath their orchard trees,
We hear, like them, the hum of bees
And rustle of the bladed corn;
We turn the pages that they read,
Their written words we linger o'er,

But in the sun they cast no shade,
No voice is heard, no sign is made,
No step is on the conscious floor!
Yet Love will dream, and Faith will trust,
(Since He who knows our need is just,)
That somehow, somewhere, meet we must.
Alas for him who never sees
The stars shine through his cypress–trees
Who, hopeless, lays his dead away,
Nor looks to see the breaking day
Across the mournful marbles play!
Who hath not learned, in hours of faith,
The truth to flesh and sense unknown,
That Life is ever lord of Death,
And Love can never lose its own!

We sped the time with stories old,
Wrought puzzles out, and riddles told,
Or stammered from our school–book lore
The Chief of Gambia's "golden shore."
How often since, when all the land
Was clay in Slavery's shaping hand,
As if a far–blown trumpet stirred
The languorous sin–sick air, I heard
Does not the voice of reason cry,
Claim the first right which Nature gave,
From the red scourge of bondage fly,
Nor deign to live a burdened slave!"
Our father rode again his ride
On Memphremagog's wooded side;
Sat down again to moose and samp
In trapper's hut and Indian camp;
Lived o'er the old idyllic ease
Beneath St. Francois' hemlock–trees;

164

Again for him the moonlight shone
On Norman cap and bodiced zone;
Again he heard the violin play
Which led the village dance away,
And mingled in its merry whirl
The grandam and the laughing girl.
Or, nearer home, our steps he led
Where Salisbury's level marshes spread
Mile—wide as flies the laden bee;
Where merry mowers, hale and strong,
Swept, scythe on scythe, their swaths along
The low green prairies of the sea.
We shared the fishing off Boar's Head,
And round the rocky Isles of Shoals
The hake—broil on the drift—wood coals;
The chowder on the sand—beach made,
Dipped by the hungry, steaming hot,
With spoons of clam—shell from the pot.
We heard the tales of witchcraft old,
And dream and sign and marvel told
To sleepy listeners as they lay
Stretched idly on the salted hay,
Adrift along the winding shores,
When favoring breezes deigned to blow
The square sail of the gundelow
And idle lay the useless oars.

Our mother, while she turned her wheel
Or run the new—knit stocking—heel,
Told how the Indian hordes came down
At midnight on Cocheco town,
And how her own great—uncle bore
His cruel scalp—mark to fourscore.
Recalling, in her fitting phrase,

So rich and picturesque and free,
(The common unrhymed poetry
Of simple life and country ways,)
The story of her early days,—
She made us welcome to her home;
Old hearths grew wide to give us room;
We stole with her a frightened look
At the gray wizard's conjuring–book,
The fame whereof went far and wide
Through all the simple country side;
We heard the hawks at twilight play,
The boat–horn on Piscataqua,
The loon's weird laughter far away;
We fished her little trout–brook, knew
What flowers in wood and meadow grew,
What sunny hillsides autumn–brown
She climbed to shake the ripe nuts down,
Saw where in sheltered cove and bay
The ducks' black squadron anchored lay,
And heard the wild–geese calling loud
Beneath the gray November cloud.

Then, haply, with a look more grave,
And soberer tone, some tale she gave
From painful Sewell's ancient tome,
Beloved in every Quaker home,
Of faith fire–winged by martyrdom,
Or Chalkley's Journal, old and quaint,—
Gentlest of skippers, rare sea–saint!—
Who, when the dreary calms prevailed,
And water–butt and bread–cask failed,
And cruel, hungry eyes pursued
His portly presence mad for food,
With dark hints muttered under breath

Of casting lots for life or death,
Offered, if Heaven withheld supplies,
To be himself the sacrifice.
Then, suddenly, as if to save
The good man from his living grave,
A ripple on the water grew,
A school of porpoise flashed in view.
"Take, eat," he said, "and be content;
These fishes in my stead are sent
By Him who gave the tangled ram
To spare the child of Abraham."

Our uncle, innocent of books,
Was rich in lore of fields and brooks,
The ancient teachers never dumb
Of Nature's unhoused lyceum.
In moons and tides and weather wise,
He read the clouds as prophecies,
And foul or fair could well divine,
By many an occult hint and sign,
Holding the cunning-warded keys
To all the woodcraft mysteries;
Himself to Nature's heart so near
That all her voices in his ear
Of beast or bird had meanings clear,
Like Apollonius of old,
Who knew the tales the sparrows told,
Or Hermes who interpreted
What the sage cranes of Nilus said;

Content to live where life began;
A simple, guileless, childlike man,

Strong only on his native grounds,
The little world of sights and sounds
Whose girdle was the parish bounds,
Whereof his fondly partial pride
The common features magnified,
As Surrey hills to mountains grew
In White of Selborne's loving view,—
He told how teal and loon he shot,
And how the eagle's eggs he got,
The feats on pond and river done,
The prodigies of rod and gun;
Till, warming with the tales he told,
Forgotten was the outside cold,
The bitter wind unheeded blew,
From ripening corn the pigeons flew,
The partridge drummed I' the wood, the mink
Went fishing down the river–brink.
In fields with bean or clover gay,
The woodchuck, like a hermit gray,
Peered from the doorway of his cell;
The muskrat plied the mason's trade,
And tier by tier his mud–walls laid;
And from the shagbark overhead
The grizzled squirrel dropped his shell.

Next, the dear aunt, whose smile of cheer
And voice in dreams I see and hear,—
The sweetest woman ever Fate
Perverse denied a household mate,
Who, lonely, homeless, not the less
Found peace in love's unselfishness,
And welcome wheresoe'er she went,
A calm and gracious element,—
Whose presence seemed the sweet income

168

And womanly atmosphere of home,—
Called up her girlhood memories,
The huskings and the apple–bees,
The sleigh–rides and the summer sails,
Weaving through all the poor details
And homespun warp of circumstance
A golden woof–thread of romance.
For well she kept her genial mood
And simple faith of maidenhood;
Before her still a cloud–land lay,
The mirage loomed across her way;
The morning dew, that dries so soon
With others, glistened at her noon;
Through years of toil and soil and care,
From glossy tress to thin gray hair,
All unprofaned she held apart
The virgin fancies of the heart.
Be shame to him of woman born
Who hath for such but thought of scorn.

There, too, our elder sister plied
Her evening task the stand beside;
A full, rich nature, free to trust,
Truthful and almost sternly just,
Impulsive, earnest, prompt to act,
And make her generous thought a fact,
Keeping with many a light disguise
The secret of self–sacrifice.
O heart sore–tried! thou hast the best
That Heaven itself could give thee,—rest,

Rest from all bitter thoughts and things!

How many a poor one's blessing went
With thee beneath the low green tent
Whose curtain never outward swings!

As one who held herself a part
Of all she saw, and let her heart
Against the household bosom lean,
Upon the motley–braided mat
Our youngest and our dearest sat,
Lifting her large, sweet, asking eyes,
Now bathed in the unfading green
And holy peace of Paradise.
Oh, looking from some heavenly hill,
Or from the shade of saintly palms,
Or silver reach of river calms,
Do those large eyes behold me still?
With me one little year ago:—
The chill weight of the winter snow
For months upon her grave has lain;
And now, when summer south–winds blow
And brier and harebell bloom again,
I tread the pleasant paths we trod,
I see the violet–sprinkled sod
Whereon she leaned, too frail and weak
The hillside flowers she loved to seek,
Yet following me where'er I went
With dark eyes full of love's content.
The birds are glad; the brier–rose fills
The air with sweetness; all the hills
Stretch green to June's unclouded sky;
But still I wait with ear and eye
For something gone which should be nigh,
A loss in all familiar things,
In flower that blooms, and bird that sings.

170

And yet, dear heart' remembering thee,
Am I not richer than of old?
Safe in thy immortality,
What change can reach the wealth I hold?
What chance can mar the pearl and gold
Thy love hath left in trust with me?
And while in life's late afternoon,
Where cool and long the shadows grow,
I walk to meet the night that soon
Shall shape and shadow overflow,
I cannot feel that thou art far,
Since near at need the angels are;
And when the sunset gates unbar,
Shall I not see thee waiting stand,
And, white against the evening star,
The welcome of thy beckoning hand?

Brisk wielder of the birch and rule,
The master of the district school
Held at the fire his favored place,
Its warm glow lit a laughing face
Fresh—hued and fair, where scarce appeared
The uncertain prophecy of beard.
He teased the mitten—blinded cat,
Played cross—pins on my uncle's hat,
Sang songs, and told us what befalls
In classic Dartmouth's college halls.
Born the wild Northern hills among,
From whence his yeoman father wrung
By patient toil subsistence scant,
Not competence and yet not want,

He early gained the power to pay
His cheerful, self–reliant way;
Could doff at ease his scholar's gown
To peddle wares from town to town;
Or through the long vacation's reach
In lonely lowland districts teach,
Where all the droll experience found
At stranger hearths in boarding round,
The moonlit skater's keen delight,
The sleigh–drive through the frosty night,
The rustic party, with its rough
Accompaniment of blind–man's–buff,
And whirling plate, and forfeits paid,
His winter task a pastime made.
Happy the snow–locked homes wherein
He tuned his merry violin,
Or played the athlete in the barn,
Or held the good dame's winding–yarn,
Or mirth–provoking versions told
Of classic legends rare and old,
Wherein the scenes of Greece and Rome
Had all the commonplace of home,
And little seemed at best the odds
'Twixt Yankee pedlers and old gods;
Where Pindus–born Arachthus took
The guise of any grist–mill brook,
And dread Olympus at his will
Became a huckleberry hill.

A careless boy that night be seemed;
But at his desk he had the look
And air of one who wisely schemed,
And hostage from the future took

In trained thought and lore of book.
Large–brained, clear–eyed, of such as he
Shall Freedom's young apostles be,
Who, following in War's bloody trail,
Shall every lingering wrong assail;
All chains from limb and spirit strike,
Uplift the black and white alike;
Scatter before their swift advance
The darkness and the ignorance,
The pride, the lust, the squalid sloth,
Which nurtured Treason's monstrous growth,
Made murder pastime, and the hell
Of prison–torture possible;
The cruel lie of caste refute,
Old forms remould, and substitute
For Slavery's lash the freeman's will,
For blind routine, wise–handed skill;
A school–house plant on every hill,
Stretching in radiate nerve–lines thence
The quick wires of intelligence;
Till North and South together brought
Shall own the same electric thought,
In peace a common flag salute,
And, side by side in labor's free
And unresentful rivalry,
Harvest the fields wherein they fought.

Another guest that winter night
Flashed back from lustrous eyes the light.
Unmarked by time, and yet not young,
The honeyed music of her tongue
And words of meekness scarcely told
A nature passionate and bold,
Strong, self–concentred, spurning guide,

Its milder features dwarfed beside
Her unbent will's majestic pride.
She sat among us, at the best,
A not unfeared, half–welcome guest,
Rebuking with her cultured phrase
Our homeliness of words and ways.
A certain pard–like, treacherous grace
Swayed the lithe limbs and dropped the lash,
Lent the white teeth their dazzling flash;
And under low brows, black with night,
Rayed out at times a dangerous light;
The sharp heat–lightnings of her face
Presaging ill to him whom Fate
Condemned to share her love or hate.
A woman tropical, intense
In thought and act, in soul and sense,
She blended in a like degree
The vixen and the devotee,
Revealing with each freak or feint
The temper of Petruchio's Kate,
The raptures of Siena's saint.
Her tapering hand and rounded wrist
Had facile power to form a fist;
The warm, dark languish of her eyes
Was never safe from wrath's surprise.
Brows saintly calm and lips devout
Knew every change of scowl and pout;
And the sweet voice had notes more high
And shrill for social battle–cry.

Since then what old cathedral town
Has missed her pilgrim staff and gown,
What convent–gate has held its lock
Against the challenge of her knock!

174

Through Smyrna's plague-hushed thoroughfares,
Up sea-set Malta's rocky stairs,
Gray olive slopes of hills that hem
Thy tombs and shrines, Jerusalem,
Or startling on her desert throne
The crazy Queen of Lebanon s
With claims fantastic as her own,
Her tireless feet have held their way;
And still, unrestful, bowed, and gray,
She watches under Eastern skies,
With hope each day renewed and fresh,
The Lord's quick coming in the flesh,
Whereof she dreams and prophesies!

Where'er her troubled path may be,
The Lord's sweet pity with her go!
The outward wayward life we see,
The hidden springs we may not know.
Nor is it given us to discern
What threads the fatal sisters spun,
Through what ancestral years has run
The sorrow with the woman born,
What forged her cruel chain of moods,
What set her feet in solitudes,
And held the love within her mute,
What mingled madness in the blood,
A life-long discord and annoy,
Water of tears with oil of joy,
And hid within the folded bud
Perversities of flower and fruit.
It is not ours to separate
The tangled skein of will and fate,
To show what metes and bounds should stand
Upon the soul's debatable land,

And between choice and Providence
Divide the circle of events;
But lie who knows our frame is just,
Merciful and compassionate,
And full of sweet assurances
And hope for all the language is,
That He remembereth we are dust!

At last the great logs, crumbling low,
Sent out a dull and duller glow,
The bull's–eye watch that hung in view,
Ticking its weary circuit through,
Pointed with mutely warning sign
Its black hand to the hour of nine.
That sign the pleasant circle broke
My uncle ceased his pipe to smoke,
Knocked from its bowl the refuse gray,
And laid it tenderly away,
Then roused himself to safely cover
The dull red brands with ashes over.
And while, with care, our mother laid
The work aside, her steps she stayed
One moment, seeking to express
Her grateful sense of happiness
For food and shelter, warmth and health,
And love's contentment more than wealth,
With simple wishes (not the weak,
Vain prayers which no fulfilment seek,
But such as warm the generous heart,
O'er–prompt to do with Heaven its part)
That none might lack, that bitter night,
For bread and clothing, warmth and light.

Poems of Nature, Poems Subjective and Reminiscent

Within our beds awhile we heard
The wind that round the gables roared,
With now and then a ruder shock,
Which made our very bedsteads rock.
We heard the loosened clapboards tost,
The board—nails snapping in the frost;
And on us, through the unplastered wall,
Felt the light sifted snow—flakes fall.
But sleep stole on, as sleep will do
When hearts are light and life is new;
Faint and more faint the murmurs grew,
Till in the summer—land of dreams
They softened to the sound of streams,
Low stir of leaves, and dip of oars,
And lapsing waves on quiet shores.

Next morn we wakened with the shout
Of merry voices high and clear;
And saw the teamsters drawing near
To break the drifted highways out.
Down the long hillside treading slow
We saw the half—buried oxen' go,
Shaking the snow from heads uptost,
Their straining nostrils white with frost.
Before our door the straggling train
Drew up, an added team to gain.
The elders threshed their hands a—cold,
Passed, with the cider—mug, their jokes
From lip to lip; the younger folks
Down the loose snow—banks, wrestling, rolled,
Then toiled again the cavalcade
O'er windy hill, through clogged ravine,
And woodland paths that wound between

Low drooping pine—boughs winter—weighed.
From every barn a team afoot,
At every house a new recruit,
Where, drawn by Nature's subtlest law
Haply the watchful young men saw
Sweet doorway pictures of the curls
And curious eyes of merry girls,
Lifting their hands in mock defence
Against the snow—ball's compliments,
And reading in each missive tost
The charm with Eden never lost.

We heard once more the sleigh—bells' sound;
And, following where the teamsters led,
The wise old Doctor went his round,
Just pausing at our door to say,
In the brief autocratic way
Of one who, prompt at Duty's call,
Was free to urge her claim on all,
That some poor neighbor sick abed
At night our mother's aid would need.
For, one in generous thought and deed,
What mattered in the sufferer's sight
The Quaker matron's inward light,
The Doctor's mail of Calvin's creed?
All hearts confess the saints elect
Who, twain in faith, in love agree,
And melt not in an acid sect
The Christian pearl of charity!

So days went on: a week had passed
Since the great world was heard from last.

The Almanac we studied o'er,
Read and reread our little store,
Of books and pamphlets, scarce a score;
One harmless novel, mostly hid
From younger eyes, a book forbid,
And poetry, (or good or bad,
A single book was all we had,)
Where Ellwood's meek, drab–skirted Muse,
A stranger to the heathen Nine,
Sang, with a somewhat nasal whine,
The wars of David and the Jews.
At last the floundering carrier bore
The village paper to our door.
Lo! broadening outward as we read,
To warmer zones the horizon spread;
In panoramic length unrolled
We saw the marvels that it told.
Before us passed the painted Creeks,
And daft McGregor on his raids
In Costa Rica's everglades.
And up Taygetos winding slow
Rode Ypsilanti's Mainote Greeks,
A Turk's head at each saddle–bow
Welcome to us its week–old news,
Its corner for the rustic Muse,
Its monthly gauge of snow and rain,
Its record, mingling in a breath
The wedding bell and dirge of death;
Jest, anecdote, and love–lorn tale,
The latest culprit sent to jail;
Its hue and cry of stolen and lost,
Its vendue sales and goods at cost,
And traffic calling loud for gain.
We felt the stir of hall and street,
The pulse of life that round us beat;
The chill embargo of the snow

Was melted in the genial glow;
Wide swung again our ice–locked door,
And all the world was ours once more!

Clasp, Angel of the backward look
And folded wings of ashen gray
And voice of echoes far away,
The brazen covers of thy book;
The weird palimpsest old and vast,
Wherein thou hid'st the spectral past;
Where, closely mingling, pale and glow
The characters of joy and woe;
The monographs of outlived years,
Or smile–illumed or dim with tears,
Green hills of life that slope to death,
And haunts of home, whose vistaed trees
Shade off to mournful cypresses
With the white amaranths underneath.
Even while I look, I can but heed
The restless sands' incessant fall,
Importunate hours that hours succeed,
Each clamorous with its own sharp need,
And duty keeping pace with all.
Shut down and clasp the heavy lids;
I hear again the voice that bids
The dreamer leave his dream midway
For larger hopes and graver fears
Life greatens in these later years,
The century's aloe flowers to–day!

Yet, haply, in some lull of life,
Some Truce of God which breaks its strife,

The worldling's eyes shall gather dew,
Dreaming in throngful city ways
Of winter joys his boyhood knew;
And dear and early friends—the few
Who yet remain—shall pause to view
These Flemish pictures of old days;
Sit with me by the homestead hearth,
And stretch the hands of memory forth
To warm them at the wood–fire's blaze!
And thanks untraced to lips unknown
Shall greet me like the odors blown
From unseen meadows newly mown,
Or lilies floating in some pond,
Wood–fringed, the wayside gaze beyond;
The traveller owns the grateful sense
Of sweetness near, he knows not whence,
And, pausing, takes with forehead bare
The benediction of the air.
1866.

MY TRIUMPH.

The autumn–time has come;
On woods that dream of bloom,
And over purpling vines,
The low sun fainter shines.

The aster–flower is failing,
The hazel's gold is paling;
Yet overhead more near
The eternal stars appear!

And present gratitude
Insures the future's good,
And for the things I see
I trust the things to be;

That in the paths untrod,
And the long days of God,
My feet shall still be led,
My heart be comforted.

O living friends who love me!
O dear ones gone above me!
Careless of other fame,
I leave to you my name.

Hide it from idle praises,
Save it from evil phrases
Why, when dear lips that spake it
Are dumb, should strangers wake it?

Let the thick curtain fall;
I better know than all
How little I have gained,
How vast the unattained.

Not by the page word–painted
Let life be banned or sainted
Deeper than written scroll
The colors of the soul.

Sweeter than any sung
My songs that found no tongue;
Nobler than any fact
My wish that failed of act.

Others shall sing the song,
Others shall right the wrong,—
Finish what I begin,
And all I fail of win.

What matter, I or they?
Mine or another's day,
So the right word be said
And life the sweeter made?

Hail to the coming singers
Hail to the brave light–bringers!
Forward I reach and share
All that they sing and dare.

The airs of heaven blow o'er me;
A glory shines before me
Of what mankind shall be,—
Pure, generous, brave, and free.

A dream of man and woman
Diviner but still human,
Solving the riddle old,
Shaping the Age of Gold.

The love of God and neighbor;
An equal-handed labor;
The richer life, where beauty
Walks hand in hand with duty.

Ring, bells in unreared steeples,
The joy of unborn peoples!
Sound, trumpets far off blown,
Your triumph is my own!

Parcel and part of all,
I keep the festival,
Fore-reach the good to be,
And share the victory.

I feel the earth move sunward,
I join the great march onward,
And take, by faith, while living,
My freehold of thanksgiving.
1870.

IN SCHOOL–DAYS.

Still sits the school–house by the road,
A ragged beggar sleeping;
Around it still the sumachs grow,
And blackberry–vines are creeping.

Within, the master's desk is seen,
Deep scarred by raps official;
The warping floor, the battered seats,
The jack–knife's carved initial;

The charcoal frescos on its wall;
Its door's worn sill, betraying
The feet that, creeping slow to school,
Went storming out to playing!

Long years ago a winter sun
Shone over it at setting;
Lit up its western window–panes,

And low eaves' icy fretting.

It touched the tangled golden curls,
And brown eyes full of grieving,
Of one who still her steps delayed
When all the school were leaving.

For near her stood the little boy
Her childish favor singled:
His cap pulled low upon a face
Where pride and shame were mingled.

Pushing with restless feet the snow
To right and left, he lingered;—
As restlessly her tiny hands
The blue–checked apron fingered.

He saw her lift her eyes; he felt
The soft hand's light caressing,
And heard the tremble of her voice,
As if a fault confessing.

"I 'm sorry that I spelt the word
I hate to go above you,
Because,"—the brown eyes lower fell,—
"Because you see, I love you!"

186

Still memory to a gray–haired man
That sweet child–face is showing.
Dear girl! the grasses on her grave
Have forty years been growing!

He lives to learn, in life's hard school,
How few who pass above him
Lament their triumph and his loss,
Like her,—because they love him.

MY BIRTHDAY.

Beneath the moonlight and the snow
Lies dead my latest year;
The winter winds are wailing low
Its dirges in my ear.

I grieve not with the moaning wind
As if a loss befell;
Before me, even as behind,
God is, and all is well!

His light shines on me from above,
His low voice speaks within,—

The patience of immortal love
Outwearying mortal sin.

Not mindless of the growing years
Of care and loss and pain,
My eyes are wet with thankful tears
For blessings which remain.

If dim the gold of life has grown,
I will not count it dross,
Nor turn from treasures still my own
To sigh for lack and loss.

The years no charm from Nature take;
As sweet her voices call,
As beautiful her mornings break,
As fair her evenings fall.

Love watches o'er my quiet ways,
Kind voices speak my name,
And lips that find it hard to praise
Are slow, at least, to blame.

How softly ebb the tides of will!
How fields, once lost or won,
Now lie behind me green and still

Beneath a level sun.

How hushed the hiss of party hate,
The clamor of the throng!
How old, harsh voices of debate
Flow into rhythmic song!

Methinks the spirit's temper grows
Too soft in this still air;
Somewhat the restful heart foregoes
Of needed watch and prayer.

The bark by tempest vainly tossed
May founder in the calm,
And he who braved the polar frost
Faint by the isles of balm.

Better than self–indulgent years
The outflung heart of youth,
Than pleasant songs in idle ears
The tumult of the truth.

Rest for the weary hands is good,
And love for hearts that pine,
But let the manly habitude
Of upright souls be mine.

Let winds that blow from heaven refresh,
Dear Lord, the languid air;
And let the weakness of the flesh
Thy strength of spirit share.

And, if the eye must fail of light,
The ear forget to hear,
Make clearer still the spirit's sight,
More fine the inward ear!

Be near me in mine hours of need
To soothe, or cheer, or warn,
And down these slopes of sunset lead
As up the hills of morn!
1871.

RED RIDING–HOOD.

On the wide lawn the snow lay deep,
Ridged o'er with many a drifted heap;
The wind that through the pine–trees sung
The naked elm–boughs tossed and swung;
While, through the window, frosty–starred,
Against the sunset purple barred,
We saw the sombre crow flap by,
The hawk's gray fleck along the sky,

The crested blue–jay flitting swift,
The squirrel poising on the drift,
Erect, alert, his broad gray tail
Set to the north wind like a sail.

It came to pass, our little lass,
With flattened face against the glass,
And eyes in which the tender dew
Of pity shone, stood gazing through
The narrow space her rosy lips
Had melted from the frost's eclipse
"Oh, see," she cried, "the poor blue–jays!
What is it that the black crow says?
The squirrel lifts his little legs
Because he has no hands, and begs;
He's asking for my nuts, I know
May I not feed them on the snow?"

Half lost within her boots, her head
Warm–sheltered in her hood of red,
Her plaid skirt close about her drawn,
She floundered down the wintry lawn;
Now struggling through the misty veil
Blown round her by the shrieking gale;
Now sinking in a drift so low
Her scarlet hood could scarcely show
Its dash of color on the snow.

She dropped for bird and beast forlorn
Her little store of nuts and corn,

And thus her timid guests bespoke
"Come, squirrel, from your hollow oak,—
Come, black old crow,—come, poor blue–jay,
Before your supper's blown away
Don't be afraid, we all are good;
And I'm mamma's Red Riding–Hood!"

O Thou whose care is over all,
Who heedest even the sparrow's fall,
Keep in the little maiden's breast
The pity which is now its guest!
Let not her cultured years make less
The childhood charm of tenderness,
But let her feel as well as know,
Nor harder with her polish grow!
Unmoved by sentimental grief
That wails along some printed leaf,
But, prompt with kindly word and deed
To own the claims of all who need,
Let the grown woman's self make good
The promise of Red Riding–Hood
1877.

RESPONSE.

On the occasion of my seventieth birthday in 1877, I was the
recipient of many tokens of esteem. The publishers of the *Atlantic
Monthly* gave a dinner in my name, and the editor of *The Literary
World* gathered in his paper many affectionate messages from my
associates in literature and the cause of human progress. The lines
which follow were written in acknowledgment.

Beside that milestone where the level sun,
Nigh unto setting, sheds his last, low rays
On word and work irrevocably done,
Life's blending threads of good and ill outspun,
I hear, O friends! your words of cheer and praise,
Half doubtful if myself or otherwise.
Like him who, in the old Arabian joke,
A beggar slept and crowned Caliph woke.
Thanks not the less. With not unglad surprise
I see my life–work through your partial eyes;
Assured, in giving to my home–taught songs
A higher value than of right belongs,
You do but read between the written lines
The finer grace of unfulfilled designs.

AT EVENTIDE.

Poor and inadequate the shadow–play
Of gain and loss, of waking and of dream,
Against life's solemn background needs must seem
At this late hour. Yet, not unthankfully,
I call to mind the fountains by the way,
The breath of flowers, the bird–song on the spray,
Dear friends, sweet human loves, the joy of giving
And of receiving, the great boon of living
In grand historic years when Liberty
Had need of word and work, quick sympathies
For all who fail and suffer, song's relief,
Nature's uncloying loveliness; and chief,
The kind restraining hand of Providence,
The inward witness, the assuring sense
Of an Eternal Good which overlies

The sorrow of the world, Love which outlives
All sin and wrong, Compassion which forgives
To the uttermost, and Justice whose clear eyes
Through lapse and failure look to the intent,
And judge our frailty by the life we meant.
1878.

VOYAGE OF THE JETTIE.

The picturesquely situated Wayside Inn at West Ossipee, N. H., is now in ashes; and to its former guests these somewhat careless rhymes may be a not unwelcome reminder of pleasant summers and autumns on the banks of the Bearcamp and Chocorua. To the author himself they have a special interest from the fact that they were written, or improvised, under the eye and for the amusement of a beloved invalid friend whose last earthly sunsets faded from the mountain ranges of Ossipee and Sandwich.

A shallow stream, from fountains
Deep in the Sandwich mountains,
Ran lake ward Bearcamp River;
And, between its flood–torn shores,
Sped by sail or urged by oars
No keel had vexed it ever.

Alone the dead trees yielding
To the dull axe Time is wielding,
The shy mink and the otter,
And golden leaves and red,
By countless autumns shed,

Had floated down its water.

From the gray rocks of Cape Ann,
Came a skilled seafaring man,
With his dory, to the right place;
Over hill and plain he brought her,
Where the boatless Beareamp water
Comes winding down from White–Face.

Quoth the skipper: "Ere she floats forth;
I'm sure my pretty boat's worth,
At least, a name as pretty."
On her painted side he wrote it,
And the flag that o'er her floated
Bore aloft the name of Jettie.

On a radiant morn of summer,
Elder guest and latest comer
Saw her wed the Bearcamp water;
Heard the name the skipper gave her,
And the answer to the favor
From the Bay State's graceful daughter.

Then, a singer, richly gifted,
Her charmed voice uplifted;
And the wood–thrush and song–sparrow
Listened, dumb with envious pain,
To the clear and sweet refrain

Whose notes they could not borrow.

Then the skipper plied his oar,
And from off the shelving shore,
Glided out the strange explorer;
Floating on, she knew not whither,—
The tawny sands beneath her,
The great hills watching o'er her.

On, where the stream flows quiet
As the meadows' margins by it,
Or widens out to borrow a
New life from that wild water,
The mountain giant's daughter,
The pine—besung Chocorua.

Or, mid the tangling cumber
And pack of mountain lumber
That spring floods downward force,
Over sunken snag, and bar
Where the grating shallows are,
The good boat held her course.

Under the pine—dark highlands,
Around the vine—hung islands,
She ploughed her crooked furrow
And her rippling and her lurches
Scared the river eels and perches,

196

And the musk–rat in his burrow.

Every sober clam below her,
Every sage and grave pearl–grower,
Shut his rusty valves the tighter;
Crow called to crow complaining,
And old tortoises sat craning
Their leathern necks to sight her.

So, to where the still lake glasses
The misty mountain masses
Rising dim and distant northward,
And, with faint–drawn shadow pictures,
Low shores, and dead pine spectres,
Blends the skyward and the earthward,

On she glided, overladen,
With merry man and maiden
Sending back their song and laughter,—
While, perchance, a phantom crew,
In a ghostly birch canoe,
Paddled dumb and swiftly after!

And the bear on Ossipee
Climbed the topmost crag to see
The strange thing drifting under;
And, through the haze of August,
Passaconaway and Paugus

Looked down in sleepy wonder.

All the pines that o'er her hung
In mimic sea–tones sung
The song familiar to her;
And the maples leaned to screen her,
And the meadow–grass seemed greener,
And the breeze more soft to woo her.

The lone stream mystery–haunted,
To her the freedom granted
To scan its every feature,
Till new and old were blended,
And round them both extended
The loving arms of Nature.

Of these hills the little vessel
Henceforth is part and parcel;
And on Bearcamp shall her log
Be kept, as if by George's
Or Grand Menan, the surges
Tossed her skipper through the fog.

And I, who, half in sadness,
Recall the morning gladness
Of life, at evening time,
By chance, onlooking idly,
Apart from all so widely,

Have set her voyage to rhyme.

Dies now the gay persistence
Of song and laugh, in distance;
Alone with me remaining
The stream, the quiet meadow,
The hills in shine and shadow,
The sombre pines complaining.

And, musing here, I dream
Of voyagers on a stream
From whence is no returning,
Under sealed orders going,
Looking forward little knowing,
Looking back with idle yearning.

And I pray that every venture
The port of peace may enter,
That, safe from snag and fall
And siren–haunted islet,
And rock, the Unseen Pilot
May guide us one and all.
1880.

MY TRUST.

A picture memory brings to me

I look across the years and see
Myself beside my mother's knee.

I feel her gentle hand restrain
My selfish moods, and know again
A child's blind sense of wrong and pain.

But wiser now, a man gray grown,
My childhood's needs are better known,
My mother's chastening love I own.

Gray grown, but in our Father's sight
A child still groping for the light
To read His works and ways aright.

I wait, in His good time to see
That as my mother dealt with me
So with His children dealeth He.

I bow myself beneath His hand
That pain itself was wisely planned
I feel, and partly understand.

The joy that comes in sorrow's guise,

The sweet pains of self—sacrifice,
I would not have them otherwise.

And what were life and death if sin
Knew not the dread rebuke within,
The pang of merciful discipline?

Not with thy proud despair of old,
Crowned stoic of Rome's noblest mould!
Pleasure and pain alike I hold.

I suffer with no vain pretence
Of triumph over flesh and sense,
Yet trust the grievous providence,

How dark soe'er it seems, may tend,
By ways I cannot comprehend,
To some unguessed benignant end;

That every loss and lapse may gain
The clear—aired heights by steps of pain,
And never cross is borne in vain.
1880.

A NAME

Addressed to my grand–nephew, Greenleaf Whittier Pickard. Jonathan
Greenleaf, in A Genealogy of the Greenleaf Family, says briefly:
"From all that can be gathered, it is believed that the ancestors
of the Greenleaf family were Huguenots, who left France on account
of their religious principles some time in the course of the
sixteenth century, and settled in England. The name was probably
translated from the French Feuillevert."

The name the Gallic exile bore,
St. Malo! from thy ancient mart,
Became upon our Western shore
Greenleaf for Feuillevert.

A name to hear in soft accord
Of leaves by light winds overrun,
Or read, upon the greening sward
Of May, in shade and sun.

The name my infant ear first heard
Breathed softly with a mother's kiss;
His mother's own, no tenderer word
My father spake than this.

No child have I to bear it on;

Be thou its keeper; let it take
From gifts well used and duty done
New beauty for thy sake.

The fair ideals that outran
My halting footsteps seek and find—
The flawless symmetry of man,
The poise of heart and mind.

Stand firmly where I felt the sway
Of every wing that fancy flew,
See clearly where I groped my way,
Nor real from seeming knew.

And wisely choose, and bravely hold
Thy faith unswerved by cross or crown,
Like the stout Huguenot of old
Whose name to thee comes down.

As Marot's songs made glad the heart
Of that lone exile, haply mine
May in life's heavy hours impart
Some strength and hope to thine.

Yet when did Age transfer to Youth
The hard–gained lessons of its day?

Each lip must learn the taste of truth,
Each foot must feel its way.

We cannot hold the hands of choice
That touch or shun life's fateful keys;
The whisper of the inward voice
Is more than homilies.

Dear boy! for whom the flowers are born,
Stars shine, and happy song–birds sing,
What can my evening give to morn,
My winter to thy spring!

A life not void of pure intent,
With small desert of praise or blame,
The love I felt, the good I meant,
I leave thee with my name.
1880.

GREETING.

Originally prefixed to the volume, The King's Missive and other
Poems.

I spread a scanty board too late;
The old–time guests for whom I wait

Come few and slow, methinks, to–day.
Ah! who could hear my messages
Across the dim unsounded seas
On which so many have sailed away!

Come, then, old friends, who linger yet,
And let us meet, as we have met,
Once more beneath this low sunshine;
And grateful for the good we 've known,
The riddles solved, the ills outgrown,
Shake bands upon the border line.

The favor, asked too oft before,
From your indulgent ears, once more
I crave, and, if belated lays
To slower, feebler measures move,
The silent, sympathy of love
To me is dearer now than praise.

And ye, O younger friends, for whom
My hearth and heart keep open room,
Come smiling through the shadows long,
Be with me while the sun goes down,
And with your cheerful voices drown
The minor of my even–song.

For, equal through the day and night,
The wise Eternal oversight

And love and power and righteous will
Remain: the law of destiny
The best for each and all must be,
And life its promise shall fulfil.
1881.

AN AUTOGRAPH.

I write my name as one,
On sands by waves o'errun
Or winter's frosted pane,
Traces a record vain.

Oblivion's blankness claims
Wiser and better names,
And well my own may pass
As from the strand or glass.

Wash on, O waves of time!
Melt, noons, the frosty rime!
Welcome the shadow vast,
The silence that shall last.

When I and all who know
And love me vanish so,
What harm to them or me
Will the lost memory be?

If any words of mine,
Through right of life divine,
Remain, what matters it
Whose hand the message writ?

Why should the "crowner's quest"
Sit on my worst or best?
Why should the showman claim
The poor ghost of my name?

Yet, as when dies a sound
Its spectre lingers round,
Haply my spent life will
Leave some faint echo still.

A whisper giving breath
Of praise or blame to death,
Soothing or saddening such
As loved the living much.

Therefore with yearnings vain
And fond I still would fain
A kindly judgment seek,
A tender thought bespeak.

And, while my words are read,
Let this at least be said
"Whate'er his life's defeatures,
He loved his fellow–creatures.

"If, of the Law's stone table,
To hold he scarce was able
The first great precept fast,
He kept for man the last.

"Through mortal lapse and dulness
What lacks the Eternal Fulness,
If still our weakness can
Love Him in loving man?

"Age brought him no despairing
Of the world's future faring;
In human nature still
He found more good than ill.

"To all who dumbly suffered,
His tongue and pen he offered;
His life was not his own,
Nor lived for self alone.

"Hater of din and riot
He lived in days unquiet;
And, lover of all beauty,
Trod the hard ways of duty.

"He meant no wrong to any
He sought the good of many,
Yet knew both sin and folly,—
May God forgive him wholly!"
1882.

ABRAM MORRISON.

'Midst the men and things which will
Haunt an old man's memory still,
Drollest, quaintest of them all,
With a boy's laugh I recall
Good old Abram Morrison.

When the Grist and Rolling Mill
Ground and rumbled by Po Hill,
And the old red school–house stood
Midway in the Powow's flood,
Here dwelt Abram Morrison.

From the Beach to far beyond

Bear–Hill, Lion's Mouth and Pond,
Marvellous to our tough old stock,
Chips o' the Anglo–Saxon block,
Seemed the Celtic Morrison.

Mudknock, Balmawhistle, all
Only knew the Yankee drawl,
Never brogue was heard till when,
Foremost of his countrymen,
Hither came Friend Morrison;

Yankee born, of alien blood,
Kin of his had well withstood
Pope and King with pike and ball
Under Derry's leaguered wall,
As became the Morrisons.

Wandering down from Nutfield woods
With his household and his goods,
Never was it clearly told
How within our quiet fold
Came to be a Morrison.

Once a soldier, blame him not
That the Quaker he forgot,
When, to think of battles won,
And the red–coats on the run,
Laughed aloud Friend Morrison.

From gray Lewis over sea
Bore his sires their family tree,
On the rugged boughs of it
Grafting Irish mirth and wit,
And the brogue of Morrison.

Half a genius, quick to plan,
Blundering like an Irishman,
But with canny shrewdness lent
By his far–off Scotch descent,
Such was Abram Morrison.

Back and forth to daily meals,
Rode his cherished pig on wheels,
And to all who came to see
"Aisier for the pig an' me,
Sure it is," said Morrison.

Simple–hearted, boy o'er–grown,
With a humor quite his own,
Of our sober–stepping ways,
Speech and look and cautious phrase,
Slow to learn was Morrison.

Much we loved his stories told

Of a country strange and old,
Where the fairies danced till dawn,
And the goblin Leprecaun
Looked, we thought, like Morrison.

Or wild tales of feud and fight,
Witch and troll and second sight
Whispered still where Stornoway
Looks across its stormy bay,
Once the home of Morrisons.

First was he to sing the praise
Of the Powow's winding ways;
And our straggling village took
City grandeur to the look
Of its poet Morrison.

All his words have perished. Shame
On the saddle–bags of Fame,
That they bring not to our time
One poor couplet of the rhyme
Made by Abram Morrison!

When, on calm and fair First Days,
Rattled down our one–horse chaise,
Through the blossomed apple–boughs
To the old, brown meeting–house,
There was Abram Morrison.

Underneath his hat's broad brim
Peered the queer old face of him;
And with Irish jauntiness
Swung the coat–tails of the dress
Worn by Abram Morrison.

Still, in memory, on his feet,
Leaning o'er the elders' seat,
Mingling with a solemn drone,
Celtic accents all his own,
Rises Abram Morrison.

"Don't," he's pleading, "don't ye go,
Dear young friends, to sight and show,
Don't run after elephants,
Learned pigs and presidents
And the likes!" said Morrison.

On his well–worn theme intent,
Simple, child–like, innocent,
Heaven forgive the half–checked smile
Of our careless boyhood, while
Listening to Friend Morrison!

We have learned in later days

Truth may speak in simplest phrase;
That the man is not the less
For quaint ways and home–spun dress,
Thanks to Abram Morrison!

Not to pander nor to please
Come the needed homilies,
With no lofty argument
Is the fitting message sent,
Through such lips as Morrison's.

Dead and gone! But while its track
Powow keeps to Merrimac,
While Po Hill is still on guard,
Looking land and ocean ward,
They shall tell of Morrison!

After half a century's lapse,
We are wiser now, perhaps,
But we miss our streets amid
Something which the past has hid,
Lost with Abram Morrison.

Gone forever with the queer
Characters of that old year
Now the many are as one;
Broken is the mould that run
Men like Abram Morrison.

1884.

A LEGACY

Friend of my many years
When the great silence falls, at last, on me,
Let me not leave, to pain and sadden thee,
A memory of tears,

But pleasant thoughts alone
Of one who was thy friendship's honored guest
And drank the wine of consolation pressed
From sorrows of thy own.

I leave with thee a sense
Of hands upheld and trials rendered less—
The unselfish joy which is to helpfulness
Its own great recompense;

The knowledge that from thine,
As from the garments of the Master, stole
Calmness and strength, the virtue which makes whole
And heals without a sign;

Yea more, the assurance strong

That love, which fails of perfect utterance here,
Lives on to fill the heavenly atmosphere
With its immortal song.
1887.

RELIGIOUS POEMS

THE STAR OF BETHLEHEM

Where Time the measure of his hours
By changeful bud and blossom keeps,
And, like a young bride crowned with flowers,
Fair Shiraz in her garden sleeps;

Where, to her poet's turban stone,
The Spring her gift of flowers imparts,
Less sweet than those his thoughts have sown
In the warm soil of Persian hearts:

There sat the stranger, where the shade
Of scattered date–trees thinly lay,
While in the hot clear heaven delayed
The long and still and weary day.

Strange trees and fruits above him hung,
Strange odors filled the sultry air,
Strange birds upon the branches swung,
Strange insect voices murmured there.

And strange bright blossoms shone around,
Turned sunward from the shadowy bowers,
As if the Gheber's soul had found
A fitting home in Iran's flowers.

Whate'er he saw, whate'er he heard,
Awakened feelings new and sad,—
No Christian garb, nor Christian word,
Nor church with Sabbath–bell chimes glad,

But Moslem graves, with turban stones,
And mosque–spires gleaming white, in view,
And graybeard Mollahs in low tones
Chanting their Koran service through.

The flowers which smiled on either hand,
Like tempting fiends, were such as they
Which once, o'er all that Eastern land,
As gifts on demon altars lay.

As if the burning eye of Baal
The servant of his Conqueror knew,
From skies which knew no cloudy veil,
The Sun's hot glances smote him through.

"Ah me!" the lonely stranger said,
"The hope which led my footsteps on,
And light from heaven around them shed,
O'er weary wave and waste, is gone!

"Where are the harvest fields all white,
For Truth to thrust her sickle in?
Where flock the souls, like doves in flight,
From the dark hiding–place of sin?

"A silent–horror broods o'er all,—
The burden of a hateful spell,—
The very flowers around recall
The hoary magi's rites of hell!

"And what am I, o'er such a land
The banner of the Cross to bear?
Dear Lord, uphold me with Thy hand,
Thy strength with human weakness share!"

He ceased; for at his very feet
In mild rebuke a floweret smiled;
How thrilled his sinking heart to greet
The Star–flower of the Virgin's child!

Sown by some wandering Frank, it drew
Its life from alien air and earth,
And told to Paynim sun and dew
The story of the Saviour's birth.

From scorching beams, in kindly mood,
The Persian plants its beauty screened,
And on its pagan sisterhood,
In love, the Christian floweret leaned.

With tears of joy the wanderer felt
The darkness of his long despair
Before that hallowed symbol melt,
Which God's dear love had nurtured there.

From Nature's face, that simple flower
The lines of sin and sadness swept;
And Magian pile and Paynim bower
In peace like that of Eden slept.

Each Moslem tomb, and cypress old,
Looked holy through the sunset air;
And, angel–like, the Muezzin told
From tower and mosque the hour of prayer.

With cheerful steps, the morrow's dawn
From Shiraz saw the stranger part;
The Star–flower of the Virgin–Born
Still blooming in his hopeful heart!
1830.

THE CITIES OF THE PLAIN

"Get ye up from the wrath of God's terrible day!
Ungirded, unsandalled, arise and away!
'T is the vintage of blood, 't is the fulness of time,
And vengeance shall gather the harvest of crime!"

The warning was spoken—the righteous had gone,
And the proud ones of Sodom were feasting alone;
All gay was the banquet—the revel was long,

With the pouring of wine and the breathing of song.

'T was an evening of beauty; the air was perfume,
The earth was all greenness, the trees were all bloom;
And softly the delicate viol was heard,
Like the murmur of love or the notes of a bird.

And beautiful maidens moved down in the dance,
With the magic of motion and sunshine of glance
And white arms wreathed lightly, and tresses fell free
As the plumage of birds in some tropical tree.

Where the shrines of foul idols were lighted on high,
And wantonness tempted the lust of the eye;
Midst rites of obsceneness, strange, loathsome, abhorred,
The blasphemer scoffed at the name of the Lord.

Hark! the growl of the thunder,—the quaking of earth!
Woe, woe to the worship, and woe to the mirth!
The black sky has opened; there's flame in the air;
The red arm of vengeance is lifted and bare!

Then the shriek of the dying rose wild where the song
And the low tone of love had been whispered along;
For the fierce flames went lightly o'er palace and bower,
Like the red tongues of demons, to blast and devour!

221

Down, down on the fallen the red ruin rained,
And the reveller sank with his wine–cup undrained;
The foot of the dancer, the music's loved thrill,
And the shout and the laughter grew suddenly still.

The last throb of anguish was fearfully given;
The last eye glared forth in its madness on Heaven!
The last groan of horror rose wildly and vain,
And death brooded over the pride of the Plain!
1831.

THE CALL OF THE CHRISTIAN

Not always as the whirlwind's rush
On Horeb's mount of fear,
Not always as the burning bush
To Midian's shepherd seer,
Nor as the awful voice which came
To Israel's prophet bards,
Nor as the tongues of cloven flame,
Nor gift of fearful words,—

Not always thus, with outward sign
Of fire or voice from Heaven,
The message of a truth divine,
The call of God is given!

Awaking in the human heart
Love for the true and right,—
Zeal for the Christian's better part,
Strength for the Christian's fight.

Nor unto manhood's heart alone
The holy influence steals
Warm with a rapture not its own,
The heart of woman feels!
As she who by Samaria's wall
The Saviour's errand sought,—
As those who with the fervent Paul
And meek Aquila wrought:

Or those meek ones whose martyrdom
Rome's gathered grandeur saw
Or those who in their Alpine home
Braved the Crusader's war,
When the green Vaudois, trembling, heard,
Through all its vales of death,
The martyr's song of triumph poured
From woman's failing breath.

And gently, by a thousand things
Which o'er our spirits pass,
Like breezes o'er the harp's fine strings,
Or vapors o'er a glass,
Leaving their token strange and new
Of music or of shade,
The summons to the right and true

And merciful is made.

Oh, then, if gleams of truth and light
Flash o'er thy waiting mind,
Unfolding to thy mental sight
The wants of human–kind;
If, brooding over human grief,
The earnest wish is known
To soothe and gladden with relief
An anguish not thine own;

Though heralded with naught of fear,
Or outward sign or show;
Though only to the inward ear
It whispers soft and low;
Though dropping, as the manna fell,
Unseen, yet from above,
Noiseless as dew–fall, heed it well,——
Thy Father's call of love!

THE CRUCIFIXION.

Sunlight upon Judha's hills!
And on the waves of Galilee;
On Jordan's stream, and on the rills
That feed the dead and sleeping sea!
Most freshly from the green wood springs
The light breeze on its scented wings;
And gayly quiver in the sun

The cedar tops of Lebanon!

A few more hours,—a change hath come!
The sky is dark without a cloud!
The shouts of wrath and joy are dumb,
And proud knees unto earth are bowed.
A change is on the hill of Death,
The helmed watchers pant for breath,
And turn with wild and maniac eyes
From the dark scene of sacrifice!

That Sacrifice!—the death of Him,—
The Christ of God, the holy One!
Well may the conscious Heaven grow dim,
And blacken the beholding, Sun.
The wonted light hath fled away,
Night settles on the middle day,
And earthquake from his caverned bed
Is waking with a thrill of dread!

The dead are waking underneath!
Their prison door is rent away!
And, ghastly with the seal of death,
They wander in the eye of day!
The temple of the Cherubim,
The House of God is cold and dim;
A curse is on its trembling walls,
Its mighty veil asunder falls!

Well may the cavern–depths of Earth
Be shaken, and her mountains nod;
Well may the sheeted dead come forth
To see the suffering son of God!
Well may the temple–shrine grow dim,
And shadows veil the Cherubim,
When He, the chosen one of Heaven,
A sacrifice for guilt is given!

And shall the sinful heart, alone,
Behold unmoved the fearful hour,
When Nature trembled on her throne,
And Death resigned his iron power?
Oh, shall the heart—whose sinfulness
Gave keenness to His sore distress,
And added to His tears of blood—
Refuse its trembling gratitude!
1834.

PALESTINE

Blest land of Judaea! thrice hallowed of song,
Where the holiest of memories pilgrim–like throng;
In the shade of thy palms, by the shores of thy sea,
On the hills of thy beauty, my heart is with thee.

With the eye of a spirit I look on that shore
Where pilgrim and prophet have lingered before;

With the glide of a spirit I traverse the sod
Made bright by the steps of the angels of God.

Blue sea of the hills! in my spirit I hear
Thy waters, Gennesaret, chime on my ear;
Where the Lowly and Just with the people sat down,
And thy spray on the dust of His sandals was thrown.

Beyond are Bethulia's mountains of green,
And the desolate hills of the wild Gadarene;
And I pause on the goat–crags of Tabor to see
The gleam of thy waters, O dark Galilee!

Hark, a sound in the valley! where, swollen and strong,
Thy river, O Kishon, is sweeping along;
Where the Canaanite strove with Jehovah in vain,
And thy torrent grew dark with the blood of the slain.

There down from his mountains stern Zebulon came,
And Naphthali's stag, with his eyeballs of flame,
And the chariots of Jabin rolled harmlessly on,
For the arm of the Lord was Abinoam's son!

There sleep the still rocks and the caverns which rang
To the song which the beautiful prophetess sang,
When the princes of Issachar stood by her side,

And the shout of a host in its triumph replied.

Lo, Bethlehem's hill—site before me is seen,
With the mountains around, and the valleys between;
There rested the shepherds of Judah, and there
The song of the angels rose sweet on the air.

And Bethany's palm—trees in beauty still throw
Their shadows at noon on the ruins below;
But where are the sisters who hastened to greet
The lowly Redeemer, and sit at His feet?

I tread where the twelve in their wayfaring trod;
I stand where they stood with the chosen of God—
Where His blessing was heard and His lessons were taught,
Where the blind were restored and the healing was wrought.

Oh, here with His flock the sad Wanderer came;
These hills He toiled over in grief are the same;
The founts where He drank by the wayside still flow,
And the same airs are blowing which breathed on His brow!

And throned on her hills sits Jerusalem yet,
But with dust on her forehead, and chains on her feet;
For the crown of her pride to the mocker hath gone,
And the holy Shechinah is dark where it shone.

But wherefore this dream of the earthly abode
Of Humanity clothed in the brightness of God?
Were my spirit but turned from the outward and dim,
It could gaze, even now, on the presence of Him!

Not in clouds and in terrors, but gentle as when,
In love and in meekness, He moved among men;
And the voice which breathed peace to the waves of the sea
In the hush of my spirit would whisper to me!

And what if my feet may not tread where He stood,
Nor my ears hear the dashing of Galilee's flood,
Nor my eyes see the cross which he bowed Him to bear,
Nor my knees press Gethsemane's garden of prayer.

Yet, Loved of the Father, Thy Spirit is near
To the meek, and the lowly, and penitent here;
And the voice of Thy love is the same even now
As at Bethany's tomb or on Olivet's brow.

Oh, the outward hath gone! but in glory and power.
The spirit surviveth the things of an hour;
Unchanged, undecaying, its Pentecost flame
On the heart's secret altar is burning the same
1837.

HYMNS.

FROM THE FRENCH OF LAMARTINE

I.
"Encore un hymne, O ma lyre
Un hymn pour le Seigneur,
Un hymne dans mon delire,
Un hymne dans mon bonheur."

One hymn more, O my lyre!
Praise to the God above,
Of joy and life and love,
Sweeping its strings of fire!

Oh, who the speed of bird and wind
And sunbeam's glance will lend to me,
That, soaring upward, I may find
My resting–place and home in Thee?
Thou, whom my soul, midst doubt and gloom,
Adoreth with a fervent flame,—
Mysterious spirit! unto whom
Pertain nor sign nor name!

Swiftly my lyre's soft murmurs go,
Up from the cold and joyless earth,
Back to the God who bade them flow,
Whose moving spirit sent them forth.
But as for me, O God! for me,
The lowly creature of Thy will,
Lingering and sad, I sigh to Thee,
An earth–bound pilgrim still!

Was not my spirit born to shine
Where yonder stars and suns are glowing?
To breathe with them the light divine
From God's own holy altar flowing?
To be, indeed, whate'er the soul
In dreams hath thirsted for so long,—
A portion of heaven's glorious whole
Of loveliness and song?

Oh, watchers of the stars at night,
Who breathe their fire, as we the air,—
Suns, thunders, stars, and rays of light,
Oh, say, is He, the Eternal, there?
Bend there around His awful throne
The seraph's glance, the angel's knee?
Or are thy inmost depths His own,
O wild and mighty sea?

Thoughts of my soul, how swift ye go!
Swift as the eagle's glance of fire,

Or arrows from the archer's bow,
To the far aim of your desire!
Thought after thought, ye thronging rise,
Like spring—doves from the startled wood,
Bearing like them your sacrifice
Of music unto God!

And shall these thoughts of joy and love
Come back again no more to me?
Returning like the patriarch's dove
Wing—weary from the eternal sea,
To bear within my longing arms
The promise—bough of kindlier skies,
Plucked from the green, immortal palms
Which shadow Paradise?

All—moving spirit! freely forth
At Thy command the strong wind goes
Its errand to the passive earth,
Nor art can stay, nor strength oppose,
Until it folds its weary wing
Once more within the hand divine;
So, weary from its wandering,
My spirit turns to Thine!

Child of the sea, the mountain stream,
From its dark caverns, hurries on,
Ceaseless, by night and morning's beam,
By evening's star and noontide's sun,
Until at last it sinks to rest,

O'erwearied, in the waiting sea,
And moans upon its mother's breast,—
So turns my soul to Thee!

O Thou who bidst the torrent flow,
Who lendest wings unto the wind,—
Mover of all things! where art Thou?
Oh, whither shall I go to find
The secret of Thy resting–place?
Is there no holy wing for me,
That, soaring, I may search the space
Of highest heaven for Thee?

Oh, would I were as free to rise
As leaves on autumn's whirlwind borne,—
The arrowy light of sunset skies,
Or sound, or ray, or star of morn,
Which melts in heaven at twilight's close,
Or aught which soars unchecked and free
Through earth and heaven; that I might lose
Myself in finding Thee!

II.
LE CRI DE L'AME.

"Quand le souffle divin qui flotte sur le monde."

When the breath divine is flowing,
Zephyr–like o'er all things going,
And, as the touch of viewless fingers,
Softly on my soul it lingers,
Open to a breath the lightest,
Conscious of a touch the slightest,—
As some calm, still lake, whereon
Sinks the snowy–bosomed swan,
And the glistening water–rings
Circle round her moving wings
When my upward gaze is turning
Where the stars of heaven are burning
Through the deep and dark abyss,
Flowers of midnight's wilderness,
Blowing with the evening's breath
Sweetly in their Maker's path
When the breaking day is flushing
All the east, and light is gushing
Upward through the horizon's haze,
Sheaf–like, with its thousand rays,
Spreading, until all above
Overflows with joy and love,
And below, on earth's green bosom,
All is changed to light and blossom:

When my waking fancies over
Forms of brightness flit and hover
Holy as the seraphs are,
Who by Zion's fountains wear
On their foreheads, white and broad,
"Holiness unto the Lord!"
When, inspired with rapture high,
It would seem a single sigh

Could a world of love create;
That my life could know no date,
And my eager thoughts could fill
Heaven and Earth, o'erflowing still!

Then, O Father! Thou alone,
From the shadow of Thy throne,
To the sighing of my breast
And its rapture answerest.
All my thoughts, which, upward winging,
Bathe where Thy own light is springing,—
All my yearnings to be free
Are at echoes answering Thee!

Seldom upon lips of mine,
Father! rests that name of Thine;
Deep within my inmost breast,
In the secret place of mind,
Like an awful presence shrined,
Doth the dread idea rest
Hushed and holy dwells it there,
Prompter of the silent prayer,
Lifting up my spirit's eye
And its faint, but earnest cry,
From its dark and cold abode,
Unto Thee, my Guide and God!
1837

THE FAMILIST'S HYMN.

The Puritans of New England, even in their wilderness home, were
not exempted from the sectarian contentions which agitated the
mother country after the downfall of Charles the First, and of the
established Episcopacy. The Quakers, Baptists, and Catholics were
banished, on pain of death, from the Massachusetts Colony. One
Samuel Gorton, a bold and eloquent declaimer, after preaching for a
time in Boston against the doctrines of the Puritans, and declaring
that their churches were mere human devices, and their sacrament
and baptism an abomination, was driven out of the jurisdiction of
the colony, and compelled to seek a residence among the savages. He
gathered round him a considerable number of converts, who, like the
primitive Christians, shared all things in common. His opinions,
however, were so troublesome to the leading clergy of the colony,
that they instigated an attack upon his "Family" by an armed force,
which seized upon the principal men in it, and brought them into
Massachusetts, where they were sentenced to be kept at hard labor
in several towns (one only in each town), during the pleasure of
the General Court, they being forbidden, under severe penalties, to
utter any of their religious sentiments, except to such ministers
as might labor for their conversion. They were unquestionably
sincere in their opinions, and, whatever may have been their
errors, deserve to be ranked among those who have in all ages
suffered for the freedom of conscience.

Father! to Thy suffering poor
Strength and grace and faith impart,
And with Thy own love restore
Comfort to the broken heart!
Oh, the failing ones confirm
With a holier strength of zeal!
Give Thou not the feeble worm
Helpless to the spoiler's heel!

Father! for Thy holy sake
We are spoiled and hunted thus;
Joyful, for Thy truth we take
Bonds and burthens unto us
Poor, and weak, and robbed of all,
Weary with our daily task,
That Thy truth may never fall
Through our weakness, Lord, we ask.

Round our fired and wasted homes
Flits the forest–bird unscared,
And at noon the wild beast comes
Where our frugal meal was shared;
For the song of praises there
Shrieks the crow the livelong day;
For the sound of evening prayer
Howls the evil beast of prey!

Sweet the songs we loved to sing
Underneath Thy holy sky;
Words and tones that used to bring
Tears of joy in every eye;
Dear the wrestling hours of prayer,
When we gathered knee to knee,
Blameless youth and hoary hair,
Bowed, O God, alone to Thee.

As Thine early children, Lord,
Shared their wealth and daily bread,

Even so, with one accord,
We, in love, each other fed.
Not with us the miser's hoard,
Not with us his grasping hand;
Equal round a common board,
Drew our meek and brother band!

Safe our quiet Eden lay
When the war–whoop stirred the land
And the Indian turned away
From our home his bloody hand.
Well that forest–ranger saw,
That the burthen and the curse
Of the white man's cruel law
Rested also upon us.

Torn apart, and driven forth
To our toiling hard and long,
Father! from the dust of earth
Lift we still our grateful song!
Grateful, that in bonds we share
In Thy love which maketh free;
Joyful, that the wrongs we bear,
Draw us nearer, Lord, to Thee!

Grateful! that where'er we toil,—
By Wachuset's wooded side,
On Nantucket's sea–worn isle,
Or by wild Neponset's tide,—
Still, in spirit, we are near,

And our evening hymns, which rise
Separate and discordant here,
Meet and mingle in the skies!

Let the scoffer scorn and mock,
Let the proud and evil priest
Rob the needy of his flock,
For his wine–cup and his feast,—
Redden not Thy bolts in store
Through the blackness of Thy skies?
For the sighing of the poor
Wilt Thou not, at length, arise?

Worn and wasted, oh! how long
Shall thy trodden poor complain?
In Thy name they bear the wrong,
In Thy cause the bonds of pain!
Melt oppression's heart of steel,
Let the haughty priesthood see,
And their blinded followers feel,
That in us they mock at Thee!

In Thy time, O Lord of hosts,
Stretch abroad that hand to save
Which of old, on Egypt's coasts,
Smote apart the Red Sea's wave
Lead us from this evil land,
From the spoiler set us free,
And once more our gathered band,
Heart to heart, shall worship Thee!

1838.

EZEKIEL

Also, thou son of man, the children of thy people still are talking
against thee by the walls and in the doors of the houses, and speak
one to another, every one to his brother, saying, Come, I pray you,
and hear what is the word that cometh forth from the Lord. And they
come unto thee as the people cometh, and they sit before thee as my
people, and they hear thy words, but they will not do them: for
with their mouth they skew much love, but their heart goeth after
their covetousness. And, lo, thou art unto them as a very lovely
song of one that hath a pleasant voice, and can play well on an
instrument: for they hear thy words, but they do them not. And when
this cometh to pass, (lo, it will come,) then shall they know that
a prophet hath been among them.—EZEKIEL, xxxiii. 30–33.

They hear Thee not, O God! nor see;
Beneath Thy rod they mock at Thee;
The princes of our ancient line
Lie drunken with Assyrian wine;
The priests around Thy altar speak
The false words which their hearers seek;
And hymns which Chaldea's wanton maids
Have sung in Dura's idol–shades
Are with the Levites' chant ascending,
With Zion's holiest anthems blending!

On Israel's bleeding bosom set,
The heathen heel is crushing yet;

The towers upon our holy hill
Echo Chaldean footsteps still.
Our wasted shrines,—who weeps for them?
Who mourneth for Jerusalem?
Who turneth from his gains away?
Whose knee with mine is bowed to pray?
Who, leaving feast and purpling cup,
Takes Zion's lamentation up?

A sad and thoughtful youth, I went
With Israel's early banishment;
And where the sullen Chebar crept,
The ritual of my fathers kept.
The water for the trench I drew,
The firstling of the flock I slew,
And, standing at the altar's side,
I shared the Levites' lingering pride,
That still, amidst her mocking foes,
The smoke of Zion's offering rose.

In sudden whirlwind, cloud and flame,
The Spirit of the Highest came!
Before mine eyes a vision passed,
A glory terrible and vast;
With dreadful eyes of living things,
And sounding sweep of angel wings,
With circling light and sapphire throne,
And flame–like form of One thereon,
And voice of that dread Likeness sent
Down from the crystal firmament!

The burden of a prophet's power
Fell on me in that fearful hour;
From off unutterable woes
The curtain of the future rose;
I saw far down the coming time
The fiery chastisement of crime;
With noise of mingling hosts, and jar
Of falling towers and shouts of war,
I saw the nations rise and fall,
Like fire—gleams on my tent's white wall.

In dream and trance, I—saw the slain
Of Egypt heaped like harvest grain.
I saw the walls of sea—born Tyre
Swept over by the spoiler's fire;
And heard the low, expiring moan
Of Edom on his rocky throne;
And, woe is me! the wild lament
From Zion's desolation sent;
And felt within my heart each blow
Which laid her holy places low.

In bonds and sorrow, day by day,
Before the pictured tile I lay;
And there, as in a mirror, saw
The coming of Assyria's war;
Her swarthy lines of spearmen pass
Like locusts through Bethhoron's grass;
I saw them draw their stormy hem
Of battle round Jerusalem;
And, listening, heard the Hebrew wail!

Blend with the victor–trump of Baal!
Who trembled at my warning word?
Who owned the prophet of the Lord?
How mocked the rude, how scoffed the vile,
How stung the Levites' scornful smile,
As o'er my spirit, dark and slow,
The shadow crept of Israel's woe
As if the angel's mournful roll
Had left its record on my soul,
And traced in lines of darkness there
The picture of its great despair!

Yet ever at the hour I feel
My lips in prophecy unseal.
Prince, priest, and Levite gather near,
And Salem's daughters haste to hear,
On Chebar's waste and alien shore,
The harp of Judah swept once more.
They listen, as in Babel's throng
The Chaldeans to the dancer's song,
Or wild sabbeka's nightly play,—
As careless and as vain as they.

. . . . .

And thus, O Prophet–bard of old,
Hast thou thy tale of sorrow told
The same which earth's unwelcome seers

Have felt in all succeeding years.
Sport of the changeful multitude,
Nor calmly heard nor understood,
Their song has seemed a trick of art,
Their warnings but, the actor's part.
With bonds, and scorn, and evil will,
The world requites its prophets still.

So was it when the Holy One
The garments of the flesh put on
Men followed where the Highest led
For common gifts of daily bread,
And gross of ear, of vision dim,
Owned not the Godlike power of Him.
Vain as a dreamer's words to them
His wail above Jerusalem,
And meaningless the watch He kept
Through which His weak disciples slept.

Yet shrink not thou, whoe'er thou art,
For God's great purpose set apart,
Before whose far–discerning eyes,
The Future as the Present lies!
Beyond a narrow–bounded age
Stretches thy prophet–heritage,
Through Heaven's vast spaces angel–trod,
And through the eternal years of God
Thy audience, worlds!—all things to be
The witness of the Truth in thee!
1844.

WHAT THE VOICE SAID

MADDENED by Earth's wrong and evil,
"Lord!" I cried in sudden ire,
"From Thy right hand, clothed with thunder,
Shake the bolted fire!

"Love is lost, and Faith is dying;
With the brute the man is sold;
And the dropping blood of labor
Hardens into gold.

"Here the dying wail of Famine,
There the battle's groan of pain;
And, in silence, smooth–faced Mammon
Reaping men like grain.

"'Where is God, that we should fear Him?'
Thus the earth–born Titans say
'God! if Thou art living, hear us!'
Thus the weak ones pray."

"Thou, the patient Heaven upbraiding,"
Spake a solemn Voice within;
"Weary of our Lord's forbearance,

Art thou free from sin?

"Fearless brow to Him uplifting,
Canst thou for His thunders call,
Knowing that to guilt's attraction
Evermore they fall?

"Know'st thou not all germs of evil
In thy heart await their time?
Not thyself, but God's restraining,
Stays their growth of crime.

"Couldst thou boast, O child of weakness!
O'er the sons of wrong and strife,
Were their strong temptations planted
In thy path of life?

"Thou hast seen two streamlets gushing
From one fountain, clear and free,
But by widely varying channels
Searching for the sea.

"Glideth one through greenest valleys,
Kissing them with lips still sweet;
One, mad roaring down the mountains,
Stagnates at their feet.

"Is it choice whereby the Parsee
Kneels before his mother's fire?
In his black tent did the Tartar
Choose his wandering sire?

"He alone, whose hand is bounding
Human power and human will,
Looking through each soul's surrounding,
Knows its good or ill.

"For thyself, while wrong and sorrow
Make to thee their strong appeal,
Coward wert thou not to utter
What the heart must feel.

"Earnest words must needs be spoken
When the warm heart bleeds or burns
With its scorn of wrong, or pity
For the wronged, by turns.

"But, by all thy nature's weakness,
Hidden faults and follies known,
Be thou, in rebuking evil,
Conscious of thine own.

"Not the less shall stern—eyed Duty
To thy lips her trumpet set,
But with harsher blasts shall mingle
Wailings of regret."

Cease not, Voice of holy speaking,
Teacher sent of God, be near,
Whispering through the day's cool silence,
Let my spirit hear!

So, when thoughts of evil—doers
Waken scorn, or hatred move,
Shall a mournful fellow—feeling
Temper all with love.
1847.

THE ANGEL OF PATIENCE.

A FREE PARAPHRASE OF THE GERMAN.

To weary hearts, to mourning homes,
God's meekest Angel gently comes
No power has he to banish pain,
Or give us back our lost again;
And yet in tenderest love, our dear
And Heavenly Father sends him here.

There's quiet in that Angel's glance,
There 's rest in his still countenance!
He mocks no grief with idle cheer,
Nor wounds with words the mourner's ear;
But ills and woes he may not cure
He kindly trains us to endure.

Angel of Patience! sent to calm
Our feverish brows with cooling palm;
To lay the storms of hope and fear,
And reconcile life's smile and tear;
The throbs of wounded pride to still,
And make our own our Father's will.

O thou who mournest on thy way,
With longings for the close of day;
He walks with thee, that Angel kind,
And gently whispers, "Be resigned
Bear up, bear on, the end shall tell
The dear Lord ordereth all things well!"
1847.

THE WIFE OF MANOAH TO HER HUSBAND.

Against the sunset's glowing wall
The city towers rise black and tall,

Where Zorah, on its rocky height,
Stands like an armed man in the light.

Down Eshtaol's vales of ripened grain
Falls like a cloud the night amain,
And up the hillsides climbing slow
The barley reapers homeward go.

Look, dearest! how our fair child's head
The sunset light hath hallowed,
Where at this olive's foot he lies,
Uplooking to the tranquil skies.

Oh, while beneath the fervent heat
Thy sickle swept the bearded wheat,
I've watched, with mingled joy and dread,
Our child upon his grassy bed.

Joy, which the mother feels alone
Whose morning hope like mine had flown,
When to her bosom, over–blessed,
A dearer life than hers is pressed.

Dread, for the future dark and still,
Which shapes our dear one to its will;
Forever in his large calm eyes,

I read a tale of sacrifice.

The same foreboding awe I felt
When at the altar's side we knelt,
And he, who as a pilgrim came,
Rose, winged and glorious, through the flame.

I slept not, though the wild bees made
A dreamlike murmuring in the shade,
And on me the warm–fingered hours
Pressed with the drowsy smell of flowers.

Before me, in a vision, rose
The hosts of Israel's scornful foes,—
Rank over rank, helm, shield, and spear,
Glittered in noon's hot atmosphere.

I heard their boast, and bitter word,
Their mockery of the Hebrew's Lord,
I saw their hands His ark assail,
Their feet profane His holy veil.

No angel down the blue space spoke,
No thunder from the still sky broke;
But in their midst, in power and awe,
Like God's waked wrath, our child I saw!

A child no more!—harsh–browed and strong,
He towered a giant in the throng,
And down his shoulders, broad and bare,
Swept the black terror of his hair.

He raised his arm—he smote amain;
As round the reaper falls the grain,
So the dark host around him fell,
So sank the foes of Israel!

Again I looked. In sunlight shone
The towers and domes of Askelon;
Priest, warrior, slave, a mighty crowd
Within her idol temple bowed.

Yet one knelt not; stark, gaunt, and blind,
His arms the massive pillars twined,—
An eyeless captive, strong with hate,
He stood there like an evil Fate.

The red shrines smoked,—the trumpets pealed
He stooped,—the giant columns reeled;
Reeled tower and fane, sank arch and wall,
And the thick dust–cloud closed o'er all!

Above the shriek, the crash, the groan
Of the fallen pride of Askelon,
I heard, sheer down the echoing sky,
A voice as of an angel cry,—

The voice of him, who at our side
Sat through the golden eventide;
Of him who, on thy altar's blaze,
Rose fire–winged, with his song of praise.

"Rejoice o'er Israel's broken chain,
Gray mother of the mighty slain!
Rejoice!" it cried, "he vanquisheth!
The strong in life is strong in death!

"To him shall Zorah's daughters raise
Through coming years their hymns of praise,
And gray old men at evening tell
Of all be wrought for Israel.

"And they who sing and they who hear
Alike shall hold thy memory dear,
And pour their blessings on thy head,
O mother of the mighty dead!"

It ceased; and though a sound I heard
As if great wings the still air stirred,
I only saw the barley sheaves
And hills half hid by olive leaves.

I bowed my face, in awe and fear,
On the dear child who slumbered near;
"With me, as with my only son,
O God," I said, "Thy will be done!"
1847.

MY SOUL AND I

Stand still, my soul, in the silent dark
I would question thee,
Alone in the shadow drear and stark
With God and me!

What, my soul, was thy errand here?
Was it mirth or ease,
Or heaping up dust from year to year?
"Nay, none of these!"

Speak, soul, aright in His holy sight
Whose eye looks still
And steadily on thee through the night

"To do His will!"

What hast thou done, O soul of mine,
That thou tremblest so?
Hast thou wrought His task, and kept the line
He bade thee go?

Aha! thou tremblest!—well I see
Thou 'rt craven grown.
Is it so hard with God and me
To stand alone?

Summon thy sunshine bravery back,
O wretched sprite!
Let me hear thy voice through this deep and black
Abysmal night.

What hast thou wrought for Right and Truth,
For God and Man,
From the golden hours of bright–eyed youth
To life's mid span?

What, silent all! art sad of cheer?
Art fearful now?
When God seemed far and men were near,
How brave wert thou!

Ah, soul of mine, thy tones I hear,
But weak and low,
Like far sad murmurs on my ear
They come and go.

I have wrestled stoutly with the Wrong,
And borne the Right
From beneath the footfall of the throng
To life and light.

"Wherever Freedom shivered a chain,
God speed, quoth I;
To Error amidst her shouting train
I gave the lie."

Ah, soul of mine! ah, soul of mine!
Thy deeds are well:
Were they wrought for Truth's sake or for thine?
My soul, pray tell.

"Of all the work my hand hath wrought
Beneath the sky,
Save a place in kindly human thought,
No gain have I."

Go to, go to! for thy very self
Thy deeds were done
Thou for fame, the miser for pelf,
Your end is one!

And where art thou going, soul of mine?
Canst see the end?
And whither this troubled life of thine
Evermore doth tend?

What daunts thee now? what shakes thee so?
My sad soul say.
"I see a cloud like a curtain low
Hang o'er my way.

"Whither I go I cannot tell
That cloud hangs black,
High as the heaven and deep as hell
Across my track.

"I see its shadow coldly enwrap
The souls before.
Sadly they enter it, step by step,
To return no more.

"They shrink, they shudder, dear God! they kneel
To Thee in prayer.
They shut their eyes on the cloud, but feel
That it still is there.

"In vain they turn from the dread Before
To the Known and Gone;
For while gazing behind them evermore
Their feet glide on.

"Yet, at times, I see upon sweet pale faces
A light begin
To tremble, as if from holy places
And shrines within.

"And at times methinks their cold lips move
With hymn and prayer,
As if somewhat of awe, but more of love
And hope were there.

"I call on the souls who have left the light
To reveal their lot;
I bend mine ear to that wall of night,
And they answer not.

"But I hear around me sighs of pain
And the cry of fear,
And a sound like the slow sad dropping of rain,
Each drop a tear!

"Ah, the cloud is dark, and day by day
I am moving thither
I must pass beneath it on my way—
God pity me!—whither?"

Ah, soul of mine! so brave and wise
In the life–storm loud,
Fronting so calmly all human eyes
In the sunlit crowd!

Now standing apart with God and me
Thou art weakness all,
Gazing vainly after the things to be
Through Death's dread wall.

But never for this, never for this
Was thy being lent;
For the craven's fear is but selfishness,
Like his merriment.

Folly and Fear are sisters twain
One closing her eyes.
The other peopling the dark inane
With spectral lies.

Know well, my soul, God's hand controls
Whate'er thou fearest;
Round Him in calmest music rolls
Whate'er thou Nearest.

What to thee is shadow, to Him is day,
And the end He knoweth,
And not on a blind and aimless way
The spirit goeth.

Man sees no future,—a phantom show
Is alone before him;
Past Time is dead, and the grasses grow,
And flowers bloom o'er him.

Nothing before, nothing behind;
The steps of Faith
Fall on the seeming void, and find
The rock beneath.

Poems of Nature, Poems Subjective and Reminiscent

The Present, the Present is all thou hast
For thy sure possessing;
Like the patriarch's angel hold it fast
Till it gives its blessing.

Why fear the night? why shrink from Death;
That phantom wan?
There is nothing in heaven or earth beneath
Save God and man.

Peopling the shadows we turn from Him
And from one another;
All is spectral and vague and dim
Save God and our brother!

Like warp and woof all destinies
Are woven fast,
Linked in sympathy like the keys
Of an organ vast.

Pluck one thread, and the web ye mar;
Break but one
Of a thousand keys, and the paining jar
Through all will run.

O restless spirit! wherefore strain
Beyond thy sphere?
Heaven and hell, with their joy and pain,
Are now and here.

Back to thyself is measured well
All thou hast given;
Thy neighbor's wrong is thy present hell,
His bliss, thy heaven.

And in life, in death, in dark and light,
All are in God's care
Sound the black abyss, pierce the deep of night,
And He is there!

All which is real now remaineth,
And fadeth never
The hand which upholds it now sustaineth
The soul forever.

Leaning on Him, make with reverent meekness
His own thy will,
And with strength from Him shall thy utter weakness
Life's task fulfil;

And that cloud itself, which now before thee
Lies dark in view,
Shall with beams of light from the inner glory
Be stricken through.

And like meadow mist through autumn's dawn
Uprolling thin,
Its thickest folds when about thee drawn
Let sunlight in.

Then of what is to be, and of what is done,
Why queriest thou?
The past and the time to be are one,
And both are now!
1847.

WORSHIP.

"Pure religion and undefiled before God and the Father is this. To
visit the fatherless and widows in, their affliction, and to keep
himself unspotted from the world."—JAMES I. 27.

The Pagan's myths through marble lips are spoken,
And ghosts of old Beliefs still flit and moan
Round fane and altar overthrown and broken,
O'er tree–grown barrow and gray ring of stone.

Blind Faith had martyrs in those old high places,
The Syrian hill grove and the Druid's wood,
With mother's offering, to the Fiend's embraces,
Bone of their bone, and blood of their own blood.

Red altars, kindling through that night of error,
Smoked with warm blood beneath the cruel eye
Of lawless Power and sanguinary Terror,
Throned on the circle of a pitiless sky;

Beneath whose baleful shadow, overcasting
All heaven above, and blighting earth below,
The scourge grew red, the lip grew pale with fasting,
And man's oblation was his fear and woe!

Then through great temples swelled the dismal moaning
Of dirge–like music and sepulchral prayer;
Pale wizard priests, o'er occult symbols droning,
Swung their white censers in the burdened air

As if the pomp of rituals, and the savor
Of gums and spices could the Unseen One please;
As if His ear could bend, with childish favor,
To the poor flattery of the organ keys!

Feet red from war–fields trod the church aisles holy,
With trembling reverence: and the oppressor there,
Kneeling before his priest, abased and lowly,
Crushed human hearts beneath his knee of prayer.

Not such the service the benignant Father
Requireth at His earthly children's hands
Not the poor offering of vain rites, but rather
The simple duty man from man demands.

For Earth He asks it: the full joy of heaven
Knoweth no change of waning or increase;
The great heart of the Infinite beats even,
Untroubled flows the river of His peace.

He asks no taper lights, on high surrounding
The priestly altar and the saintly grave,
No dolorous chant nor organ music sounding,
Nor incense clouding tip the twilight nave.

For he whom Jesus loved hath truly spoken
The holier worship which he deigns to bless
Restores the lost, and binds the spirit broken,
And feeds the widow and the fatherless!

Types of our human weakness and our sorrow!
Who lives unhaunted by his loved ones dead?
Who, with vain longing, seeketh not to borrow
From stranger eyes the home lights which have fled?

O brother man! fold to thy heart thy brother;
Where pity dwells, the peace of God is there;
To worship rightly is to love each other,
Each smile a hymn, each kindly deed a prayer.

Follow with reverent steps the great example
Of Him whose holy work was "doing good;"
So shall the wide earth seem our Father's temple,
Each loving life a psalm of gratitude.

Then shall all shackles fall; the stormy clangor
Of wild war music o'er the earth shall cease;
Love shall tread out the baleful fire of anger,
And in its ashes plant the tree of peace!
1848.

THE HOLY LAND

Paraphrased from the lines in Lamartine's *Adieu to Marseilles*,
beginning

Poems of Nature, Poems Subjective and Reminiscent

"Je n'ai pas navigue sur l'ocean de sable."

I have not felt, o'er seas of sand,
The rocking of the desert bark;
Nor laved at Hebron's fount my hand,
By Hebron's palm–trees cool and dark;
Nor pitched my tent at even–fall,
On dust where Job of old has lain,
Nor dreamed beneath its canvas wall,
The dream of Jacob o'er again.

One vast world–page remains unread;
How shine the stars in Chaldea's sky,
How sounds the reverent pilgrim's tread,
How beats the heart with God so nigh
How round gray arch and column lone
The spirit of the old time broods,
And sighs in all the winds that moan
Along the sandy solitudes!

In thy tall cedars, Lebanon,
I have not heard the nations' cries,
Nor seen thy eagles stooping down
Where buried Tyre in ruin lies.
The Christian's prayer I have not said
In Tadmor's temples of decay,
Nor startled, with my dreary tread,
The waste where Memnon's empire lay.

Nor have I, from thy hallowed tide,
O Jordan! heard the low lament,
Like that sad wail along thy side
Which Israel's mournful prophet sent!
Nor thrilled within that grotto lone
Where, deep in night, the Bard of Kings
Felt hands of fire direct his own,
And sweep for God the conscious strings.

I have not climbed to Olivet,
Nor laid me where my Saviour lay,
And left His trace of tears as yet
By angel eyes unwept away;
Nor watched, at midnight's solemn time,
The garden where His prayer and groan,
Wrung by His sorrow and our crime,
Rose to One listening ear alone.

I have not kissed the rock–hewn grot
Where in His mother's arms He lay,
Nor knelt upon the sacred spot
Where last His footsteps pressed the clay;
Nor looked on that sad mountain head,
Nor smote my sinful breast, where wide
His arms to fold the world He spread,
And bowed His head to bless—and died!
1848.

THE REWARD

Who, looking backward from his manhood's prime,
Sees not the spectre of his misspent time?
And, through the shade
Of funeral cypress planted thick behind,
Hears no reproachful whisper on the wind
From his loved dead?

Who bears no trace of passion's evil force?
Who shuns thy sting, O terrible Remorse?
Who does not cast
On the thronged pages of his memory's book,
At times, a sad and half–reluctant look,
Regretful of the past?

Alas! the evil which we fain would shun
We do, and leave the wished–for good undone
Our strength to–day
Is but to–morrow's weakness, prone to fall;
Poor, blind, unprofitable servants all
Are we alway.

Yet who, thus looking backward o'er his years,
Feels not his eyelids wet with grateful tears,
If he hath been
Permitted, weak and sinful as he was,

To cheer and aid, in some ennobling cause,
His fellow–men?

If he hath hidden the outcast, or let in
A ray of sunshine to the cell of sin;
If he hath lent
Strength to the weak, and, in an hour of need,
Over the suffering, mindless of his creed
Or home, hath bent;

He has not lived in vain, and while he gives
The praise to Him, in whom he moves and lives,
With thankful heart;
He gazes backward, and with hope before,
Knowing that from his works he nevermore
Can henceforth part.
1848.

THE WISH OF TO–DAY.

I ask not now for gold to gild
With mocking shine a weary frame;
The yearning of the mind is stilled,
I ask not now for Fame.

A rose–cloud, dimly seen above,
Melting in heaven's blue depths away;

Oh, sweet, fond dream of human Love
For thee I may not pray.

But, bowed in lowliness of mind,
I make my humble wishes known;
I only ask a will resigned,
O Father, to Thine own!

To—day, beneath Thy chastening eye
I crave alone for peace and rest,
Submissive in Thy hand to lie,
And feel that it is best.

A marvel seems the Universe,
A miracle our Life and Death;
A mystery which I cannot pierce,
Around, above, beneath.

In vain I task my aching brain,
In vain the sage's thought I scan,
I only feel how weak and vain,
How poor and blind, is man.

And now my spirit sighs for home,
And longs for light whereby to see,
And, like a weary child, would come,

O Father, unto Thee!

Though oft, like letters traced on sand,
My weak resolves have passed away,
In mercy lend Thy helping hand
Unto my prayer to–day!
1848.

ALL'S WELL

The clouds, which rise with thunder, slake
Our thirsty souls with rain;
The blow most dreaded falls to break
From off our limbs a chain;
And wrongs of man to man but make
The love of God more plain.
As through the shadowy lens of even
The eye looks farthest into heaven
On gleams of star and depths of blue
The glaring sunshine never knew!
1850.

INVOCATION

Through Thy clear spaces, Lord, of old,
Formless and void the dead earth rolled;
Deaf to Thy heaven's sweet music, blind
To the great lights which o'er it shined;
No sound, no ray, no warmth, no breath,—

A dumb despair, a wandering death.

To that dark, weltering horror came
Thy spirit, like a subtle flame,—
A breath of life electrical,
Awakening and transforming all,
Till beat and thrilled in every part
The pulses of a living heart.

Then knew their bounds the land and sea;
Then smiled the bloom of mead and tree;
From flower to moth, from beast to man,
The quick creative impulse ran;
And earth, with life from thee renewed,
Was in thy holy eyesight good.

As lost and void, as dark and cold
And formless as that earth of old;
A wandering waste of storm and night,
Midst spheres of song and realms of light;
A blot upon thy holy sky,
Untouched, unwarned of thee, am I.

O Thou who movest on the deep
Of spirits, wake my own from sleep
Its darkness melt, its coldness warm,
The lost restore, the ill transform,
That flower and fruit henceforth may be

Its grateful offering, worthy Thee.
1851.

QUESTIONS OF LIFE

And the angel that was sent unto me, whose name was Uriel,
gave me an answer and said,
"Thy heart hath gone too far in this world, and thinkest thou
to comprehend the way of the Most High?"
Then said I, "Yea, my Lord."
Then said he unto me, "Go thy way, weigh me the weight of
the fire or measure me the blast of the wind, or call me again the
day that is past."—2 ESDRAS, chap. iv.

A bending staff I would not break,
A feeble faith I would not shake,
Nor even rashly pluck away
The error which some truth may stay,
Whose loss might leave the soul without
A shield against the shafts of doubt.

And yet, at times, when over all
A darker mystery seems to fall,
(May God forgive the child of dust,
Who seeks to know, where Faith should trust!)
I raise the questions, old and dark,
Of Uzdom's tempted patriarch,
And, speech–confounded, build again
The baffled tower of Shinar's plain.

I am: how little more I know!
Whence came I? Whither do I go?
A centred self, which feels and is;
A cry between the silences;
A shadow—birth of clouds at strife
With sunshine on the hills of life;
A shaft from Nature's quiver cast
Into the Future from the Past;
Between the cradle and the shroud,
A meteor's flight from cloud to cloud.

Thorough the vastness, arching all,
I see the great stars rise and fall,
The rounding seasons come and go,
The tided oceans ebb and flow;
The tokens of a central force,
Whose circles, in their widening course,
O'erlap and move the universe;
The workings of the law whence springs
The rhythmic harmony of things,
Which shapes in earth the darkling spar,
And orbs in heaven the morning star.
Of all I see, in earth and sky,—
Star, flower, beast, bird,—what part have I?
This conscious life,—is it the same
Which thrills the universal frame,
Whereby the caverned crystal shoots,
And mounts the sap from forest roots,
Whereby the exiled wood—bird tells
When Spring makes green her native dells?
How feels the stone the pang of birth,
Which brings its sparkling prism forth?
The forest—tree the throb which gives

The life—blood to its new—born leaves?
Do bird and blossom feel, like me,
Life's many—folded mystery,—
The wonder which it is to be?
Or stand I severed and distinct,
From Nature's "chain of life" unlinked?
Allied to all, yet not the less
Prisoned in separate consciousness,
Alone o'erburdened with a sense
Of life, and cause, and consequence?

In vain to me the Sphinx propounds
The riddle of her sights and sounds;
Back still the vaulted mystery gives
The echoed question it receives.
What sings the brook? What oracle
Is in the pine—tree's organ swell?
What may the wind's low burden be?
The meaning of the moaning sea?
The hieroglyphics of the stars?
Or clouded sunset's crimson bars?
I vainly ask, for mocks my skill
The trick of Nature's cipher still.

I turn from Nature unto men,
I ask the stylus and the pen;
What sang the bards of old? What meant
The prophets of the Orient?
The rolls of buried Egypt, hid
In painted tomb and pyramid?
What mean Idumea's arrowy lines,
Or dusk Elora's monstrous signs?

Poems of Nature, Poems Subjective and Reminiscent

How speaks the primal thought of man
From the grim carvings of Copan?

Where rests the secret? Where the keys
Of the old death—bolted mysteries?
Alas! the dead retain their trust;
Dust hath no answer from the dust.

The great enigma still unguessed,
Unanswered the eternal quest;
I gather up the scattered rays
Of wisdom in the early days,
Faint gleams and broken, like the light
Of meteors in a northern night,
Betraying to the darkling earth
The unseen sun which gave them birth;
I listen to the sibyl's chant,
The voice of priest and hierophant;
I know what Indian Kreeshna saith,
And what of life and what of death
The demon taught to Socrates;
And what, beneath his garden—trees
Slow pacing, with a dream—like tread,—
The solemn—thoughted Plato said;
Nor lack I tokens, great or small,
Of God's clear light in each and all,
While holding with more dear regard
The scroll of Hebrew seer and bard,
The starry pages promise—lit
With Christ's Evangel over—writ,
Thy miracle of life and death,
O Holy One of Nazareth!

On Aztec ruins, gray and lone,
The circling serpent coils in stone,—
Type of the endless and unknown;
Whereof we seek the clue to find,
With groping fingers of the blind!
Forever sought, and never found,
We trace that serpent–symbol round
Our resting–place, our starting bound
Oh, thriftlessness of dream and guess!
Oh, wisdom which is foolishness!
Why idly seek from outward things
The answer inward silence brings?
Why stretch beyond our proper sphere
And age, for that which lies so near?
Why climb the far–off hills with pain,
A nearer view of heaven to gain?
In lowliest depths of bosky dells
The hermit Contemplation dwells.
A fountain's pine–hung slope his seat,
And lotus–twined his silent feet,
Whence, piercing heaven, with screened sight,
He sees at noon the stars, whose light
Shall glorify the coining night.

Here let me pause, my quest forego;
Enough for me to feel and know
That He in whom the cause and end,
The past and future, meet and blend,—
Who, girt with his Immensities,
Our vast and star–hung system sees,
Small as the clustered Pleiades,—

Moves not alone the heavenly quires,
But waves the spring–time's grassy spires,
Guards not archangel feet alone,
But deigns to guide and keep my own;
Speaks not alone the words of fate
Which worlds destroy, and worlds create,
But whispers in my spirit's ear,
In tones of love, or warning fear,
A language none beside may hear.

To Him, from wanderings long and wild,
I come, an over–wearied child,
In cool and shade His peace to find,
Lice dew–fall settling on my mind.
Assured that all I know is best,
And humbly trusting for the rest,
I turn from Fancy's cloud–built scheme,
Dark creed, and mournful eastern dream
Of power, impersonal and cold,
Controlling all, itself controlled,
Maker and slave of iron laws,
Alike the subject and the cause;
From vain philosophies, that try
The sevenfold gates of mystery,
And, baffled ever, babble still,
Word–prodigal of fate and will;
From Nature, and her mockery, Art;
And book and speech of men apart,
To the still witness in my heart;
With reverence waiting to behold
His Avatar of love untold,
The Eternal Beauty new and old!
1862.

FIRST–DAY THOUGHTS.

In calm and cool and silence, once again
I find my old accustomed place among
My brethren, where, perchance, no human tongue
Shall utter words; where never hymn is sung,
Nor deep–toned organ blown, nor censer swung,
Nor dim light falling through the pictured pane!
There, syllabled by silence, let me hear
The still small voice which reached the prophet's ear;
Read in my heart a still diviner law
Than Israel's leader on his tables saw!
There let me strive with each besetting sin,
Recall my wandering fancies, and restrain
The sore disquiet of a restless brain;
And, as the path of duty is made plain,
May grace be given that I may walk therein,
Not like the hireling, for his selfish gain,
With backward glances and reluctant tread,
Making a merit of his coward dread,
But, cheerful, in the light around me thrown,
Walking as one to pleasant service led;
Doing God's will as if it were my own,
Yet trusting not in mine, but in His strength alone!
1852.

TRUST.

The same old baffling questions! O my friend,
I cannot answer them. In vain I send
My soul into the dark, where never burn

The lamps of science, nor the natural light
Of Reason's sun and stars! I cannot learn
Their great and solemn meanings, nor discern
The awful secrets of the eyes which turn
Evermore on us through the day and night
With silent challenge and a dumb demand,
Proffering the riddles of the dread unknown,
Like the calm Sphinxes, with their eyes of stone,
Questioning the centuries from their veils of sand!
I have no answer for myself or thee,
Save that I learned beside my mother's knee;
"All is of God that is, and is to be;
And God is good." Let this suffice us still,
Resting in childlike trust upon His will
Who moves to His great ends unthwarted by the ill.
1853.

TRINITAS.

At morn I prayed, "I fain would see
How Three are One, and One is Three;
Read the dark riddle unto me."

I wandered forth, the sun and air
I saw bestowed with equal care
On good and evil, foul and fair.

No partial favor dropped the rain;
Alike the righteous and profane

Rejoiced above their heading grain.

And my heart murmured, "Is it meet
That blindfold Nature thus should treat
With equal hand the tares and wheat?"

A presence melted through my mood,—
A warmth, a light, a sense of good,
Like sunshine through a winter wood.

I saw that presence, mailed complete
In her white innocence, pause to greet
A fallen sister of the street.

Upon her bosom snowy pure
The lost one clung, as if secure
From inward guilt or outward lure.

"Beware!" I said; "in this I see
No gain to her, but loss to thee
Who touches pitch defiled must be."

I passed the haunts of shame and sin,
And a voice whispered, "Who therein

Shall these lost souls to Heaven's peace win?

"Who there shall hope and health dispense,
And lift the ladder up from thence
Whose rounds are prayers of penitence?"

I said, "No higher life they know;
These earth—worms love to have it so.
Who stoops to raise them sinks as low."

That night with painful care I read
What Hippo's saint and Calvin said;
The living seeking to the dead!

In vain I turned, in weary quest,
Old pages, where (God give them rest!)
The poor creed—mongers dreamed and guessed.

And still I prayed, "Lord, let me see
How Three are One, and One is Three;
Read the dark riddle unto me!"

Then something whispered, "Dost thou pray
For what thou hast? This very day

The Holy Three have crossed thy way.

"Did not the gifts of sun and air
To good and ill alike declare
The all–compassionate Father's care?

"In the white soul that stooped to raise
The lost one from her evil ways,
Thou saw'st the Christ, whom angels praise!

"A bodiless Divinity,
The still small Voice that spake to thee
Was the Holy Spirit's mystery!

"O blind of sight, of faith how small!
Father, and Son, and Holy Call
This day thou hast denied them all!

"Revealed in love and sacrifice,
The Holiest passed before thine eyes,
One and the same, in threefold guise.

"The equal Father in rain and sun,
His Christ in the good to evil done,

His Voice in thy soul;—and the Three are One!"

I shut my grave Aquinas fast;
The monkish gloss of ages past,
The schoolman's creed aside I cast.

And my heart answered, "Lord, I see
How Three are One, and One is Three;
Thy riddle hath been read to me!"
1858.

THE SISTERS

A PICTURE BY BARRY

The shade for me, but over thee
The lingering sunshine still;
As, smiling, to the silent stream
Comes down the singing rill.

So come to me, my little one,—
My years with thee I share,
And mingle with a sister's love
A mother's tender care.

But keep the smile upon thy lip,
The trust upon thy brow;
Since for the dear one God hath called
We have an angel now.

Our mother from the fields of heaven
Shall still her ear incline;
Nor need we fear her human love
Is less for love divine.

The songs are sweet they sing beneath
The trees of life so fair,
But sweetest of the songs of heaven
Shall be her children's prayer.

Then, darling, rest upon my breast,
And teach my heart to lean
With thy sweet trust upon the arm
Which folds us both unseen!
1858

"THE ROCK" IN EL GHOR.

Dead Petra in her hill–tomb sleeps,
Her stones of emptiness remain;
Around her sculptured mystery sweeps

The lonely waste of Edom's plain.

From the doomed dwellers in the cleft
The bow of vengeance turns not back;
Of all her myriads none are left
Along the Wady Mousa's track.

Clear in the hot Arabian day
Her arches spring, her statues climb;
Unchanged, the graven wonders pay
No tribute to the spoiler, Time!

Unchanged the awful lithograph
Of power and glory undertrod;
Of nations scattered like the chaff
Blown from the threshing–floor of God.

Yet shall the thoughtful stranger turn
From Petra's gates with deeper awe,
To mark afar the burial urn
Of Aaron on the cliffs of Hor;

And where upon its ancient guard
Thy Rock, El Ghor, is standing yet,—
Looks from its turrets desertward,
And keeps the watch that God has set.

The same as when in thunders loud
It heard the voice of God to man,
As when it saw in fire and cloud
The angels walk in Israel's van,

Or when from Ezion–Geber's way
It saw the long procession file,
And heard the Hebrew timbrels play
The music of the lordly Nile;

Or saw the tabernacle pause,
Cloud–bound, by Kadesh Barnea's wells,
While Moses graved the sacred laws,
And Aaron swung his golden bells.

Rock of the desert, prophet–sung!
How grew its shadowing pile at length,
A symbol, in the Hebrew tongue,
Of God's eternal love and strength.

On lip of bard and scroll of seer,
From age to age went down the name,
Until the Shiloh's promised year,
And Christ, the Rock of Ages, came!

The path of life we walk to–day
Is strange as that the Hebrews trod;
We need the shadowing rock, as they,—
We need, like them, the guides of God.

God send His angels, Cloud and Fire,
To lead us o'er the desert sand!
God give our hearts their long desire,
His shadow in a weary land!
1859.

THE OVER–HEART.

"For of Him, and through Him, and to Him are all things,
to whom be glory forever! "—PAUL.

Above, below, in sky and sod,
In leaf and spar, in star and man,
Well might the wise Athenian scan
The geometric signs of God,
The measured order of His plan.

And India's mystics sang aright
Of the One Life pervading all,—
One Being's tidal rise and fall
In soul and form, in sound and sight,—
Eternal outflow and recall.

God is: and man in guilt and fear
The central fact of Nature owns;
Kneels, trembling, by his altar–stones,
And darkly dreams the ghastly smear
Of blood appeases and atones.

Guilt shapes the Terror: deep within
The human heart the secret lies
Of all the hideous deities;
And, painted on a ground of sin,
The fabled gods of torment rise!

And what is He? The ripe grain nods,
The sweet dews fall, the sweet flowers blow;
But darker signs His presence show
The earthquake and the storm are God's,
And good and evil interflow.

O hearts of love! O souls that turn
Like sunflowers to the pure and best!
To you the truth is manifest:
For they the mind of Christ discern
Who lean like John upon His breast!

In him of whom the sibyl told,

For whom the prophet's harp was toned,
Whose need the sage and magian owned,
The loving heart of God behold,
The hope for which the ages groaned!

Fade, pomp of dreadful imagery
Wherewith mankind have deified
Their hate, and selfishness, and pride!
Let the scared dreamer wake to see
The Christ of Nazareth at his side!

What doth that holy Guide require?
No rite of pain, nor gift of blood,
But man a kindly brotherhood,
Looking, where duty is desire,
To Him, the beautiful and good.

Gone be the faithlessness of fear,
And let the pitying heaven's sweet rain
Wash out the altar's bloody stain;
The law of Hatred disappear,
The law of Love alone remain.

How fall the idols false and grim!
And to! their hideous wreck above
The emblems of the Lamb and Dove!
Man turns from God, not God from him;
And guilt, in suffering, whispers Love!

The world sits at the feet of Christ,
Unknowing, blind, and unconsoled;
It yet shall touch His garment's fold,
And feel the heavenly Alchemist
Transform its very dust to gold.

The theme befitting angel tongues
Beyond a mortal's scope has grown.
O heart of mine! with reverence own
The fulness which to it belongs,
And trust the unknown for the known.
1859.

THE SHADOW AND THE LIGHT.

"And I sought, whence is Evil: I set before the eye of my spirit
the whole creation; whatsoever we see therein,—sea, earth, air,
stars, trees, moral creatures,—yea, whatsoever there is we do not
see,—angels and spiritual powers. Where is evil, and whence comes
it, since God the Good hath created all things? Why made He
anything at all of evil, and not rather by His Almightiness cause
it not to be? These thoughts I turned in my miserable heart,
overcharged with most gnawing cares." "And, admonished to return to
myself, I entered even into my inmost soul, Thou being my guide,
and beheld even beyond my soul and mind the Light unchangeable. He
who knows the Truth knows what that Light is, and he that knows it
knows Eternity! O—Truth, who art Eternity! Love, who art Truth!
Eternity, who art Love! And I beheld that Thou madest all things
good, and to Thee is nothing whatsoever evil. From the angel to the

worm, from the first motion to the last, Thou settest each in its
place, and everything is good in its kind. Woe is me!—how high art
Thou in the highest, how deep in the deepest! and Thou never
departest from us and we scarcely return to Thee."
—AUGUSTINE'S Soliloquies, Book VII.

The fourteen centuries fall away
Between us and the Afric saint,
And at his side we urge, to-day,
The immemorial quest and old complaint.

No outward sign to us is given,—
From sea or earth comes no reply;
Hushed as the warm Numidian heaven
He vainly questioned bends our frozen sky.

No victory comes of all our strife,—
From all we grasp the meaning slips;
The Sphinx sits at the gate of life,
With the old question on her awful lips.

In paths unknown we hear the feet
Of fear before, and guilt behind;
We pluck the wayside fruit, and eat
Ashes and dust beneath its golden rind.

From age to age descends unchecked
The sad bequest of sire to son,
The body's taint, the mind's defect;
Through every web of life the dark threads run.

Oh, why and whither? God knows all;
I only know that He is good,
And that whatever may befall
Or here or there, must be the best that could.

Between the dreadful cherubim
A Father's face I still discern,
As Moses looked of old on Him,
And saw His glory into goodness turn!

For He is merciful as just;
And so, by faith correcting sight,
I bow before His will, and trust
Howe'er they seem He doeth all things right.

And dare to hope that Tie will make
The rugged smooth, the doubtful plain;
His mercy never quite forsake;
His healing visit every realm of pain;

That suffering is not His revenge
Upon His creatures weak and frail,
Sent on a pathway new and strange
With feet that wander and with eyes that fail;

That, o'er the crucible of pain,
Watches the tender eye of Love
The slow transmuting of the chain
Whose links are iron below to gold above!

Ah me! we doubt the shining skies,
Seen through our shadows of offence,
And drown with our poor childish cries
The cradle–hymn of kindly Providence.

And still we love the evil cause,
And of the just effect complain
We tread upon life's broken laws,
And murmur at our self–inflicted pain;

We turn us from the light, and find
Our spectral shapes before us thrown,
As they who leave the sun behind
Walk in the shadows of themselves alone.

And scarce by will or strength of ours
We set our faces to the day;
Weak, wavering, blind, the Eternal Powers
Alone can turn us from ourselves away.

Our weakness is the strength of sin,
But love must needs be stronger far,
Outreaching all and gathering in
The erring spirit and the wandering star.

A Voice grows with the growing years;
Earth, hushing down her bitter cry,
Looks upward from her graves, and hears,
"The Resurrection and the Life am I."

O Love Divine!—whose constant beam
Shines on the eyes that will not see,
And waits to bless us, while we dream
Thou leavest us because we turn from thee!

All souls that struggle and aspire,
All hearts of prayer by thee are lit;
And, dim or clear, thy tongues of fire
On dusky tribes and twilight centuries sit.

Nor bounds, nor clime, nor creed thou know'st,
Wide as our need thy favors fall;
The white wings of the Holy Ghost
Stoop, seen or unseen, o'er the heads of all.

O Beauty, old yet ever new!
Eternal Voice, and Inward Word,
The Logos of the Greek and Jew,
The old sphere—music which the Samian heard!

Truth, which the sage and prophet saw,
Long sought without, but found within,
The Law of Love beyond all law,
The Life o'erflooding mortal death and sin!

Shine on us with the light which glowed
Upon the trance—bound shepherd's way.
Who saw the Darkness overflowed
And drowned by tides of everlasting Day.

Shine, light of God!—make broad thy scope
To all who sin and suffer; more
And better than we dare to hope
With Heaven's compassion make our longings poor!
1860.

THE CRY OF A LOST SOUL.

Lieutenant Herndon's Report of the Exploration of the Amazon has a
striking description of the peculiar and melancholy notes of a
bird heard by night on the shores of the river. The Indian guides
called it "The Cry of a Lost Soul"! Among the numerous translations
of this poem is one by the Emperor of Brazil.

In that black forest, where, when day is done,
With a snake's stillness glides the Amazon
Darkly from sunset to the rising sun,

A cry, as of the pained heart of the wood,
The long, despairing moan of solitude
And darkness and the absence of all good,

Startles the traveller, with a sound so drear,
So full of hopeless agony and fear,
His heart stands still and listens like his ear.

The guide, as if he heard a dead–bell toll,
Starts, drops his oar against the gunwale's thole,
Crosses himself, and whispers, "A lost soul!"

"No, Senor, not a bird. I know it well,—
It is the pained soul of some infidel
Or cursed heretic that cries from hell.

"Poor fool! with hope still mocking his despair,
He wanders, shrieking on the midnight air
For human pity and for Christian prayer.

"Saints strike him dumb! Our Holy Mother hath
No prayer for him who, sinning unto death,
Burns always in the furnace of God's wrath!"

Thus to the baptized pagan's cruel lie,
Lending new horror to that mournful cry,
The voyager listens, making no reply.

Dim burns the boat–lamp: shadows deepen round,
From giant trees with snake–like creepers wound,
And the black water glides without a sound.

But in the traveller's heart a secret sense
Of nature plastic to benign intents,
And an eternal good in Providence,

Lifts to the starry calm of heaven his eyes;
And to! rebuking all earth's ominous cries,
The Cross of pardon lights the tropic skies!

"Father of all!" he urges his strong plea,
"Thou lovest all: Thy erring child may be
Lost to himself, but never lost to Thee!

"All souls are Thine; the wings of morning bear
None from that Presence which is everywhere,
Nor hell itself can hide, for Thou art there.

"Through sins of sense, perversities of will,
Through doubt and pain, through guilt and shame and ill,
Thy pitying eye is on Thy creature still.

"Wilt thou not make, Eternal Source and Goal!
In Thy long years, life's broken circle whole,
And change to praise the cry of a lost soul?"
1862.

ANDREW RYKMAN'S PRAYER

Andrew Rykman's dead and gone;

You can see his leaning slate
In the graveyard, and thereon
Read his name and date.

"Trust is truer than our fears,"
Runs the legend through the moss,
"Gain is not in added years,
Nor in death is loss."

Still the feet that thither trod,
All the friendly eyes are dim;
Only Nature, now, and God
Have a care for him.

There the dews of quiet fall,
Singing birds and soft winds stray:
Shall the tender Heart of all
Be less kind than they?

What he was and what he is
They who ask may haply find,
If they read this prayer of his
Which he left behind.

. . . .

Pardon, Lord, the lips that dare
Shape in words a mortal's prayer!
Prayer, that, when my day is done,
And I see its setting sun,
Shorn and beamless, cold and dim,
Sink beneath the horizon's rim,—
When this ball of rock and clay
Crumbles from my feet away,
And the solid shores of sense
Melt into the vague immense,
Father! I may come to Thee
Even with the beggar's plea,
As the poorest of Thy poor,
With my needs, and nothing more.

Not as one who seeks his home
With a step assured I come;
Still behind the tread I hear
Of my life–companion, Fear;
Still a shadow deep and vast
From my westering feet is cast,
Wavering, doubtful, undefined,
Never shapen nor outlined
From myself the fear has grown,
And the shadow is my own.

Yet, O Lord, through all a sense

Of Thy tender providence
Stays my failing heart on Thee,
And confirms the feeble knee;
And, at times, my worn feet press
Spaces of cool quietness,
Lilied whiteness shone upon
Not by light of moon or sun.
Hours there be of inmost calm,
Broken but by grateful psalm,
When I love Thee more than fear Thee,
And Thy blessed Christ seems near me,
With forgiving look, as when
He beheld the Magdalen.
Well I know that all things move
To the spheral rhythm of love,—
That to Thee, O Lord of all!
Nothing can of chance befall
Child and seraph, mote and star,
Well Thou knowest what we are
Through Thy vast creative plan
Looking, from the worm to man,
There is pity in Thine eyes,
But no hatred nor surprise.
Not in blind caprice of will,
Not in cunning sleight of skill,
Not for show of power, was wrought
Nature's marvel in Thy thought.
Never careless hand and vain
Smites these chords of joy and pain;
No immortal selfishness
Plays the game of curse and bless
Heaven and earth are witnesses
That Thy glory goodness is.

Not for sport of mind and force
Hast Thou made Thy universe,
But as atmosphere and zone
Of Thy loving heart alone.
Man, who walketh in a show,
Sees before him, to and fro,
Shadow and illusion go;
All things flow and fluctuate,
Now contract and now dilate.
In the welter of this sea,
Nothing stable is but Thee;
In this whirl of swooning trance,
Thou alone art permanence;
All without Thee only seems,
All beside is choice of dreams.
Never yet in darkest mood
Doubted I that Thou wast good,
Nor mistook my will for fate,
Pain of sin for heavenly hate,—
Never dreamed the gates of pearl
Rise from out the burning marl,
Or that good can only live
Of the bad conservative,
And through counterpoise of hell
Heaven alone be possible.

For myself alone I doubt;
All is well, I know, without;
I alone the beauty mar,
I alone the music jar.
Yet, with hands by evil stained,
And an ear by discord pained,
I am groping for the keys

Of the heavenly harmonies;
Still within my heart I bear
Love for all things good and fair.
Hands of want or souls in pain
Have not sought my door in vain;
I have kept my fealty good
To the human brotherhood;
Scarcely have I asked in prayer
That which others might not share.
I, who hear with secret shame
Praise that paineth more than blame,
Rich alone in favors lent,
Virtuous by accident,
Doubtful where I fain would rest,
Frailest where I seem the best,
Only strong for lack of test,—
What am I, that I should press
Special pleas of selfishness,
Coolly mounting into heaven
On my neighbor unforgiven?
Ne'er to me, howe'er disguised,
Comes a saint unrecognized;
Never fails my heart to greet
Noble deed with warmer beat;
Halt and maimed, I own not less
All the grace of holiness;
Nor, through shame or self–distrust,
Less I love the pure and just.
Lord, forgive these words of mine
What have I that is not Thine?
Whatsoe'er I fain would boast
Needs Thy pitying pardon most.
Thou, O Elder Brother! who
In Thy flesh our trial knew,
Thou, who hast been touched by these
Our most sad infirmities,

Thou alone the gulf canst span
In the dual heart of man,
And between the soul and sense
Reconcile all difference,
Change the dream of me and mine
For the truth of Thee and Thine,
And, through chaos, doubt, and strife,
Interfuse Thy calm of life.
Haply, thus by Thee renewed,
In Thy borrowed goodness good,
Some sweet morning yet in God's
Dim, veonian periods,
Joyful I shall wake to see
Those I love who rest in Thee,
And to them in Thee allied
Shall my soul be satisfied.

Scarcely Hope hath shaped for me
What the future life may be.
Other lips may well be bold;
Like the publican of old,
I can only urge the plea,
"Lord, be merciful to me!"
Nothing of desert I claim,
Unto me belongeth shame.
Not for me the, crowns of gold,
Palms, and harpings manifold;
Not for erring eye and feet
Jasper wall and golden street.
What thou wilt, O Father, give I
All is gain that I receive.

If my voice I may not raise
In the elders' song of praise,
If I may not, sin–defiled,
Claim my birthright as a child,
Suffer it that I to Thee
As an hired servant be;
Let the lowliest task be mine,
Grateful, so the work be Thine;
Let me find the humblest place
In the shadow of Thy grace
Blest to me were any spot
Where temptation whispers not.
If there be some weaker one,
Give me strength to help him on
If a blinder soul there be,
Let me guide him nearer Thee.
Make my mortal dreams come true
With the work I fain would do;
Clothe with life the weak intent,
Let me be the thing I meant;
Let me find in Thy employ
Peace that dearer is than joy;
Out of self to love be led
And to heaven acclimated,
Until all things sweet and good
Seem my natural habitude.

. . . .

So we read the prayer of him
Who, with John of Labadie,
Trod, of old, the oozy rim

Of the Zuyder Zee.

Thus did Andrew Rykman pray.
Are we wiser, better grown,
That we may not, in our day,
Make his prayer our own?

THE ANSWER.

Spare me, dread angel of reproof,
And let the sunshine weave to–day
Its gold–threads in the warp and woof
Of life so poor and gray.

Spare me awhile; the flesh is weak.
These lingering feet, that fain would stray
Among the flowers, shall some day seek
The strait and narrow way.

Take off thy ever–watchful eye,
The awe of thy rebuking frown;
The dullest slave at times must sigh
To fling his burdens down;

To drop his galley's straining oar,

And press, in summer warmth and calm,
The lap of some enchanted shore
Of blossom and of balm.

Grudge not my life its hour of bloom,
My heart its taste of long desire;
This day be mine: be those to come
As duty shall require.

The deep voice answered to my own,
Smiting my selfish prayers away;
"To—morrow is with God alone,
And man hath but to—day.

"Say not, thy fond, vain heart within,
The Father's arm shall still be wide,
When from these pleasant ways of sin
Thou turn'st at eventide.

"'Cast thyself down,' the tempter saith,
'And angels shall thy feet upbear.'
He bids thee make a lie of faith,
And blasphemy of prayer.

"Though God be good and free be heaven,
No force divine can love compel;

And, though the song of sins forgiven
May sound through lowest hell,

"The sweet persuasion of His voice
Respects thy sanctity of will.
He giveth day: thou hast thy choice
To walk in darkness still;

"As one who, turning from the light,
Watches his own gray shadow fall,
Doubting, upon his path of night,
If there be day at all!

"No word of doom may shut thee out,
No wind of wrath may downward whirl,
No swords of fire keep watch about
The open gates of pearl;

"A tenderer light than moon or sun,
Than song of earth a sweeter hymn,
May shine and sound forever on,
And thou be deaf and dim.

"Forever round the Mercy—seat
The guiding lights of Love shall burn;
But what if, habit—bound, thy feet

Shall lack the will to turn?

"What if thine eye refuse to see,
Thine ear of Heaven's free welcome fail,
And thou a willing captive be,
Thyself thy own dark jail?

"Oh, doom beyond the saddest guess,
As the long years of God unroll,
To make thy dreary selfishness
The prison of a soul!

"To doubt the love that fain would break
The fetters from thy self–bound limb;
And dream that God can thee forsake
As thou forsakest Him!"
1863.

THE ETERNAL GOODNESS.

O friends! with whom my feet have trod
The quiet aisles of prayer,
Glad witness to your zeal for God
And love of man I bear.

I trace your lines of argument;
Your logic linked and strong
I weigh as one who dreads dissent,
And fears a doubt as wrong.

But still my human hands are weak
To hold your iron creeds
Against the words ye bid me speak
My heart within me pleads.

Who fathoms the Eternal Thought?
Who talks of scheme and plan?
The Lord is God! He needeth not
The poor device of man.

I walk with bare, hushed feet the ground
Ye tread with boldness shod;
I dare not fix with mete and bound
The love and power of God.

Ye praise His justice; even such
His pitying love I deem
Ye seek a king; I fain would touch
The robe that hath no seam.

Ye see the curse which overbroods
A world of pain and loss;
I hear our Lord's beatitudes
And prayer upon the cross.

More than your schoolmen teach, within
Myself, alas! I know
Too dark ye cannot paint the sin,
Too small the merit show.

I bow my forehead to the dust,
I veil mine eyes for shame,
And urge, in trembling self–distrust,
A prayer without a claim.

I see the wrong that round me lies,
I feel the guilt within;
I hear, with groan and travail–cries,
The world confess its sin.

Yet, in the maddening maze of things,
And tossed by storm and flood,
To one fixed trust my spirit clings;
I know that God is good!

Not mine to look where cherubim
And seraphs may not see,
But nothing can be good in Him
Which evil is in me.

The wrong that pains my soul below
I dare not throne above,
I know not of His hate,—I know
His goodness and His love.

I dimly guess from blessings known
Of greater out of sight,
And, with the chastened Psalmist, own
His judgments too are right.

I long for household voices gone,
For vanished smiles I long,
But God hath led my dear ones on,
And He can do no wrong.

I know not what the future hath
Of marvel or surprise,
Assured alone that life and death
His mercy underlies.

And if my heart and flesh are weak
To bear an untried pain,
The bruised reed He will not break,
But strengthen and sustain.

No offering of my own I have,
Nor works my faith to prove;
I can but give the gifts He gave,
And plead His love for love.

And so beside the Silent Sea
I wait the muffled oar;
No harm from Him can come to me
On ocean or on shore.

I know not where His islands lift
Their fronded palms in air;
I only know I cannot drift
Beyond His love and care.

O brothers! if my faith is vain,
If hopes like these betray,
Pray for me that my feet may gain
The sure and safer way.

And Thou, O Lord! by whom are seen
Thy creatures as they be,
Forgive me if too close I lean
My human heart on Thee!
1865.

THE COMMON QUESTION.

Behind us at our evening meal
The gray bird ate his fill,
Swung downward by a single claw,
And wiped his hooked bill.

He shook his wings and crimson tail,
And set his head aslant,
And, in his sharp, impatient way,
Asked, "What does Charlie want?"

"Fie, silly bird!" I answered, "tuck
Your head beneath your wing,
And go to sleep;"—but o'er and o'er
He asked the self–same thing.

Then, smiling, to myself I said
How like are men and birds!
We all are saying what he says,

In action or in words.

The boy with whip and top and drum,
The girl with hoop and doll,
And men with lands and houses, ask
The question of Poor Poll.

However full, with something more
We fain the bag would cram;
We sigh above our crowded nets
For fish that never swam.

No bounty of indulgent Heaven
The vague desire can stay;
Self—love is still a Tartar mill
For grinding prayers alway.

The dear God hears and pities all;
He knoweth all our wants;
And what we blindly ask of Him
His love withholds or grants.

And so I sometimes think our prayers
Might well be merged in one;
And nest and perch and hearth and church
Repeat, "Thy will be done."

317

OUR MASTER.

Immortal Love, forever full,
Forever flowing free,
Forever shared, forever whole,
A never–ebbing sea!

Our outward lips confess the name
All other names above;
Love only knoweth whence it came
And comprehendeth love.

Blow, winds of God, awake and blow
The mists of earth away!
Shine out, O Light Divine, and show
How wide and far we stray!

Hush every lip, close every book,
The strife of tongues forbear;
Why forward reach, or backward look,
For love that clasps like air?

We may not climb the heavenly steeps
To bring the Lord Christ down
In vain we search the lowest deeps,

For Him no depths can drown.

Nor holy bread, nor blood of grape,
The lineaments restore
Of Him we know in outward shape
And in the flesh no more.

He cometh not a king to reign;
The world's long hope is dim;
The weary centuries watch in vain
The clouds of heaven for Him.

Death comes, life goes; the asking eye
And ear are answerless;
The grave is dumb, the hollow sky
Is sad with silentness.

The letter fails, and systems fall,
And every symbol wanes;
The Spirit over-brooding all
Eternal Love remains.

And not for signs in heaven above
Or earth below they look,
Who know with John His smile of love,
With Peter His rebuke.

319

In joy of inward peace, or sense
Of sorrow over sin,
He is His own best evidence,
His witness is within.

No fable old, nor mythic lore,
Nor dream of bards and seers,
No dead fact stranded on the shore
Of the oblivious years;—

But warm, sweet, tender, even yet
A present help is He;
And faith has still its Olivet,
And love its Galilee.

The healing of His seamless dress
Is by our beds of pain;
We touch Him in life's throng and press,
And we are whole again.

Through Him the first fond prayers are said
Our lips of childhood frame,
The last low whispers of our dead
Are burdened with His name.

Our Lord and Master of us all!
Whate'er our name or sign,
We own Thy sway, we hear Thy call,
We test our lives by Thine.

Thou judgest us; Thy purity
Doth all our lusts condemn;
The love that draws us nearer Thee
Is hot with wrath to them.

Our thoughts lie open to Thy sight;
And, naked to Thy glance,
Our secret sins are in the light
Of Thy pure countenance.

Thy healing pains, a keen distress
Thy tender light shines in;
Thy sweetness is the bitterness,
Thy grace the pang of sin.

Yet, weak and blinded though we be,
Thou dost our service own;
We bring our varying gifts to Thee,
And Thou rejectest none.

To Thee our full humanity,
Its joys and pains, belong;
The wrong of man to man on Thee
Inflicts a deeper wrong.

Who hates, hates Thee, who loves becomes
Therein to Thee allied;
All sweet accords of hearts and homes
In Thee are multiplied.

Deep strike Thy roots, O heavenly Vine,
Within our earthly sod,
Most human and yet most divine,
The flower of man and God!

O Love! O Life! Our faith and sight
Thy presence maketh one
As through transfigured clouds of white
We trace the noon–day sun.

So, to our mortal eyes subdued,
Flesh–veiled, but not concealed,
We know in Thee the fatherhood
And heart of God revealed.

We faintly hear, we dimly see,
In differing phrase we pray;
But, dim or clear, we own in Thee
The Light, the Truth, the Way!

The homage that we render Thee
Is still our Father's own;
No jealous claim or rivalry
Divides the Cross and Throne.

To do Thy will is more than praise,
As words are less than deeds,
And simple trust can find Thy ways
We miss with chart of creeds.

No pride of self Thy service hath,
No place for me and mine;
Our human strength is weakness, death
Our life, apart from Thine.

Apart from Thee all gain is loss,
All labor vainly done;
The solemn shadow of Thy Cross
Is better than the sun.

Alone, O Love ineffable!
Thy saving name is given;
To turn aside from Thee is hell,
To walk with Thee is heaven!

How vain, secure in all Thou art,
Our noisy championship
The sighing of the contrite heart
Is more than flattering lip.

Not Thine the bigot's partial plea,
Nor Thine the zealot's ban;
Thou well canst spare a love of Thee
Which ends in hate of man.

Our Friend, our Brother, and our Lord,
What may Thy service be?—
Nor name, nor form, nor ritual word,
But simply following Thee.

We bring no ghastly holocaust,
We pile no graven stone;
He serves thee best who loveth most
His brothers and Thy own.

Thy litanies, sweet offices
Of love and gratitude;
Thy sacramental liturgies,
The joy of doing good.

In vain shall waves of incense drift
The vaulted nave around,
In vain the minster turret lift
Its brazen weights of sound.

The heart must ring Thy Christmas bells,
Thy inward altars raise;
Its faith and hope Thy canticles,
And its obedience praise!
1866.

THE MEETING.

The two speakers in the meeting referred to in this poem were Avis
Keene, whose very presence was a benediction, a woman lovely in
spirit and person, whose words seemed a message of love and tender
concern to her hearers; and Sibyl Jones, whose inspired eloquence
and rare spirituality impressed all who knew her. In obedience to
her apprehended duty she made visits of Christian love to various
parts of Europe, and to the West Coast of Africa and Palestine.

The elder folks shook hands at last,

Down seat by seat the signal passed.
To simple ways like ours unused,
Half solemnized and half amused,
With long–drawn breath and shrug, my guest
His sense of glad relief expressed.
Outside, the hills lay warm in sun;
The cattle in the meadow–run
Stood half–leg deep; a single bird
The green repose above us stirred.
"What part or lot have you," he said,
"In these dull rites of drowsy–head?
Is silence worship? Seek it where
It soothes with dreams the summer air,
Not in this close and rude–benched hall,
But where soft lights and shadows fall,
And all the slow, sleep–walking hours
Glide soundless over grass and flowers!
From time and place and form apart,
Its holy ground the human heart,
Nor ritual–bound nor templeward
Walks the free spirit of the Lord!
Our common Master did not pen
His followers up from other men;
His service liberty indeed,
He built no church, He framed no creed;
But while the saintly Pharisee
Made broader his phylactery,
As from the synagogue was seen
The dusty–sandalled Nazarene
Through ripening cornfields lead the way
Upon the awful Sabbath day,
His sermons were the healthful talk
That shorter made the mountain–walk,
His wayside texts were flowers and birds,
Where mingled with His gracious words
The rustle of the tamarisk–tree

And ripple—wash of Galilee."

"Thy words are well, O friend," I said;
"Unmeasured and unlimited,
With noiseless slide of stone to stone,
The mystic Church of God has grown.
Invisible and silent stands
The temple never made with hands,
Unheard the voices still and small
Of its unseen confessional.
He needs no special place of prayer
Whose hearing ear is everywhere;
He brings not back the childish days
That ringed the earth with stones of praise,
Roofed Karnak's hall of gods, and laid
The plinths of Phil e's colonnade.
Still less He owns the selfish good
And sickly growth of solitude,—
The worthless grace that, out of sight,
Flowers in the desert anchorite;
Dissevered from the suffering whole,
Love hath no power to save a soul.
Not out of Self, the origin
And native air and soil of sin,
The living waters spring and flow,
The trees with leaves of healing grow.

"Dream not, O friend, because I seek
This quiet shelter twice a week,
I better deem its pine—laid floor
Than breezy hill or sea—sung shore;
But nature is not solitude

She crowds us with her thronging wood;
Her many hands reach out to us,
Her many tongues are garrulous;
Perpetual riddles of surprise
She offers to our ears and eyes;
She will not leave our senses still,
But drags them captive at her will
And, making earth too great for heaven,
She hides the Giver in the given.

"And so, I find it well to come
For deeper rest to this still room,
For here the habit of the soul
Feels less the outer world's control;
The strength of mutual purpose pleads
More earnestly our common needs;
And from the silence multiplied
By these still forms on either side,
The world that time and sense have known
Falls off and leaves us God alone.

"Yet rarely through the charmed repose
Unmixed the stream of motive flows,
A flavor of its many springs,
The tints of earth and sky it brings;
In the still waters needs must be
Some shade of human sympathy;
And here, in its accustomed place,
I look on memory's dearest face;
The blind by–sitter guesseth not
What shadow haunts that vacant spot;
No eyes save mine alone can see

The love wherewith it welcomes me!
And still, with those alone my kin,
In doubt and weakness, want and sin,
I bow my head, my heart I bare
As when that face was living there,
And strive (too oft, alas! in vain)
The peace of simple trust to gain,
Fold fancy's restless wings, and lay
The idols of my heart away.

"Welcome the silence all unbroken,
Nor less the words of fitness spoken,—
Such golden words as hers for whom
Our autumn flowers have just made room;
Whose hopeful utterance through and through
The freshness of the morning blew;
Who loved not less the earth that light
Fell on it from the heavens in sight,
But saw in all fair forms more fair
The Eternal beauty mirrored there.
Whose eighty years but added grace
And saintlier meaning to her face,—
The look of one who bore away
Glad tidings from the hills of day,
While all our hearts went forth to meet
The coming of her beautiful feet!
Or haply hers, whose pilgrim tread
Is in the paths where Jesus led;
Who dreams her childhood's Sabbath dream
By Jordan's willow—shaded stream,
And, of the hymns of hope and faith,
Sung by the monks of Nazareth,
Hears pious echoes, in the call
To prayer, from Moslem minarets fall,

Repeating where His works were wrought
The lesson that her Master taught,
Of whom an elder Sibyl gave,
The prophecies of Cuma 's cave.

"I ask no organ's soulless breath
To drone the themes of life and death,
No altar candle—lit by day,
No ornate wordsman's rhetoric—play,
No cool philosophy to teach
Its bland audacities of speech
To double—tasked idolaters
Themselves their gods and worshippers,
No pulpit hammered by the fist
Of loud—asserting dogmatist,
Who borrows for the Hand of love
The smoking thunderbolts of Jove.
I know how well the fathers taught,
What work the later schoolmen wrought;
I reverence old—time faith and men,
But God is near us now as then;
His force of love is still unspent,
His hate of sin as imminent;
And still the measure of our needs
Outgrows the cramping bounds of creeds;
The manna gathered yesterday
Already savors of decay;
Doubts to the world's child—heart unknown
Question us now from star and stone;
Too little or too much we know,
And sight is swift and faith is slow;
The power is lost to self—deceive
With shallow forms of make—believe.
W e walk at high noon, and the bells

Call to a thousand oracles,
But the sound deafens, and the light
Is stronger than our dazzled sight;
The letters of the sacred Book
Glimmer and swim beneath our look;
Still struggles in the Age's breast
With deepening agony of quest
The old entreaty: 'Art thou He,
Or look we for the Christ to be?'

"God should be most where man is least
So, where is neither church nor priest,
And never rag of form or creed
To clothe the nakedness of need,—
Where farmer–folk in silence meet,—
I turn my bell–unsummoned feet;'
I lay the critic's glass aside,
I tread upon my lettered pride,
And, lowest–seated, testify
To the oneness of humanity;
Confess the universal want,
And share whatever Heaven may grant.
He findeth not who seeks his own,
The soul is lost that's saved alone.
Not on one favored forehead fell
Of old the fire–tongued miracle,
But flamed o'er all the thronging host
The baptism of the Holy Ghost;
Heart answers heart: in one desire
The blending lines of prayer aspire;
'Where, in my name, meet two or three,'
Our Lord hath said, 'I there will be!'

"So sometimes comes to soul and sense
The feeling which is evidence
That very near about us lies
The realm of spiritual mysteries.
The sphere of the supernal powers
Impinges on this world of ours.
The low and dark horizon lifts,
To light the scenic terror shifts;
The breath of a diviner air
Blows down the answer of a prayer
That all our sorrow, pain, and doubt
A great compassion clasps about,
And law and goodness, love and force,
Are wedded fast beyond divorce.
Then duty leaves to love its task,
The beggar Self forgets to ask;
With smile of trust and folded hands,
The passive soul in waiting stands
To feel, as flowers the sun and dew,
The One true Life its own renew.

"So, to the calmly gathered thought
The innermost of truth is taught,
The mystery dimly understood,
That love of God is love of good,
And, chiefly, its divinest trace
In Him of Nazareth's holy face;
That to be saved is only this,—
Salvation from our selfishness,
From more than elemental fire,
The soul's unsanetified desire,
From sin itself, and not the pain
That warns us of its chafing chain;

332

That worship's deeper meaning lies
In mercy, and not sacrifice,
Not proud humilities of sense
And posturing of penitence,
But love's unforced obedience;
That Book and Church and Day are given
For man, not God,—for earth, not heaven,—
The blessed means to holiest ends,
Not masters, but benignant friends;
That the dear Christ dwells not afar,
The king of some remoter star,
Listening, at times, with flattered ear
To homage wrung from selfish fear,
But here, amidst the poor and blind,
The bound and suffering of our kind,
In works we do, in prayers we pray,
Life of our life, He lives to–day."
1868.

THE CLEAR VISION.

I did but dream. I never knew
What charms our sternest season wore.
Was never yet the sky so blue,
Was never earth so white before.
Till now I never saw the glow
Of sunset on yon hills of snow,
And never learned the bough's designs
Of beauty in its leafless lines.

Did ever such a morning break

As that my eastern windows see?
Did ever such a moonlight take
Weird photographs of shrub and tree?
Rang ever bells so wild and fleet
The music of the winter street?
Was ever yet a sound by half
So merry as you school–boy's laugh?

O Earth! with gladness overfraught,
No added charm thy face hath found;
Within my heart the change is wrought,
My footsteps make enchanted ground.
From couch of pain and curtained room
Forth to thy light and air I come,
To find in all that meets my eyes
The freshness of a glad surprise.

Fair seem these winter days, and soon
Shall blow the warm west–winds of spring,
To set the unbound rills in tune
And hither urge the bluebird's wing.
The vales shall laugh in flowers, the woods
Grow misty green with leafing buds,
And violets and wind–flowers sway
Against the throbbing heart of May.

Break forth, my lips, in praise, and own
The wiser love severely kind;
Since, richer for its chastening grown,
I see, whereas I once was blind.

The world, O Father! hath not wronged
With loss the life by Thee prolonged;
But still, with every added year,
More beautiful Thy works appear!

As Thou hast made thy world without,
Make Thou more fair my world within;
Shine through its lingering clouds of doubt;
Rebuke its haunting shapes of sin;
Fill, brief or long, my granted span
Of life with love to thee and man;
Strike when thou wilt the hour of rest,
But let my last days be my best!
2d mo., 1868.

DIVINE COMPASSION.

Long since, a dream of heaven I had,
And still the vision haunts me oft;
I see the saints in white robes clad,
The martyrs with their palms aloft;
But hearing still, in middle song,
The ceaseless dissonance of wrong;
And shrinking, with hid faces, from the strain
Of sad, beseeching eyes, full of remorse and pain.

The glad song falters to a wail,
The harping sinks to low lament;
Before the still unlifted veil

I see the crowned foreheads bent,
Making more sweet the heavenly air,
With breathings of unselfish prayer;
And a Voice saith: "O Pity which is pain,
O Love that weeps, fill up my sufferings which remain!

"Shall souls redeemed by me refuse
To share my sorrow in their turn?
Or, sin–forgiven, my gift abuse
Of peace with selfish unconcern?
Has saintly ease no pitying care?
Has faith no work, and love no prayer?
While sin remains, and souls in darkness dwell,
Can heaven itself be heaven, and look unmoved on hell?"

Then through the Gates of Pain, I dream,
A wind of heaven blows coolly in;
Fainter the awful discords seem,
The smoke of torment grows more thin,
Tears quench the burning soil, and thence
Spring sweet, pale flowers of penitence
And through the dreary realm of man's despair,
Star–crowned an angel walks, and to! God's hope is there!

Is it a dream? Is heaven so high
That pity cannot breathe its air?
Its happy eyes forever dry,
Its holy lips without a prayer!
My God! my God! if thither led
By Thy free grace unmerited,

No crown nor palm be mine, but let me keep
A heart that still can feel, and eyes that still can weep.
1868.

THE PRAYER–SEEKER.

Along the aisle where prayer was made,
A woman, all in black arrayed,
Close–veiled, between the kneeling host,
With gliding motion of a ghost,
Passed to the desk, and laid thereon
A scroll which bore these words alone,
Pray for me!

Back from the place of worshipping
She glided like a guilty thing
The rustle of her draperies, stirred
By hurrying feet, alone was heard;
While, full of awe, the preacher read,
As out into the dark she sped:
"Pray for me!"

Back to the night from whence she came,
To unimagined grief or shame!
Across the threshold of that door
None knew the burden that she bore;
Alone she left the written scroll,
The legend of a troubled soul,—
Pray for me!

Glide on, poor ghost of woe or sin!
Thou leav'st a common need within;
Each bears, like thee, some nameless weight,
Some misery inarticulate,
Some secret sin, some shrouded dread,
Some household sorrow all unsaid.
Pray for us!

Pass on! The type of all thou art,
Sad witness to the common heart!
With face in veil and seal on lip,
In mute and strange companionship,
Like thee we wander to and fro,
Dumbly imploring as we go
Pray for us!

Ah, who shall pray, since he who pleads
Our want perchance hath greater needs?
Yet they who make their loss the gain
Of others shall not ask in vain,
And Heaven bends low to hear the prayer
Of love from lips of self–despair
Pray for us!

In vain remorse and fear and hate
Beat with bruised bands against a fate
Whose walls of iron only move

And open to the touch of love.
He only feels his burdens fall
Who, taught by suffering, pities all.
Pray for us!

He prayeth best who leaves unguessed
The mystery of another's breast.
Why cheeks grow pale, why eyes o'erflow,
Or heads are white, thou need'st not know.
Enough to note by many a sign
That every heart hath needs like thine.
Pray for us!
1870

THE BREWING OF SOMA.

"These libations mixed with milk have been prepared for Indra:
offer Soma to the drinker of Soma."
—Vashista, translated by MAX MULLER.

The fagots blazed, the caldron's smoke
Up through the green wood curled;
"Bring honey from the hollow oak,
Bring milky sap," the brewers spoke,
In the childhood of the world.

And brewed they well or brewed they ill,
The priests thrust in their rods,

First tasted, and then drank their fill,
And shouted, with one voice and will,
"Behold the drink of gods!"

They drank, and to! in heart and brain
A new, glad life began;
The gray of hair grew young again,
The sick man laughed away his pain,
The cripple leaped and ran.

"Drink, mortals, what the gods have sent,
Forget your long annoy."
So sang the priests. From tent to tent
The Soma's sacred madness went,
A storm of drunken joy.

Then knew each rapt inebriate
A winged and glorious birth,
Soared upward, with strange joy elate,
Beat, with dazed head, Varuna's gate,
And, sobered, sank to earth.

The land with Soma's praises rang;
On Gihon's banks of shade
Its hymns the dusky maidens sang;
In joy of life or mortal pang
All men to Soma prayed.

The morning twilight of the race
Sends down these matin psalms;
And still with wondering eyes we trace
The simple prayers to Soma's grace,
That Vedic verse embalms.

As in that child–world's early year,
Each after age has striven
By music, incense, vigils drear,
And trance, to bring the skies more near,
Or lift men up to heaven!

Some fever of the blood and brain,
Some self–exalting spell,
The scourger's keen delight of pain,
The Dervish dance, the Orphic strain,
The wild–haired Bacchant's yell,—

The desert's hair–grown hermit sunk
The saner brute below;
The naked Santon, hashish–drunk,
The cloister madness of the monk,
The fakir's torture–show!

And yet the past comes round again,
And new doth old fulfil;
In sensual transports wild as vain

We brew in many a Christian fane
The heathen Soma still!

Dear Lord and Father of mankind,
Forgive our foolish ways!
Reclothe us in our rightful mind,
In purer lives Thy service find,
In deeper reverence, praise.

In simple trust like theirs who heard
Beside the Syrian sea
The gracious calling of the Lord,
Let us, like them, without a word,
Rise up and follow Thee.

O Sabbath rest by Galilee!
O calm of hills above,
Where Jesus knelt to share with Thee
The silence of eternity
Interpreted by love!

With that deep hush subduing all
Our words and works that drown
The tender whisper of Thy call,
As noiseless let Thy blessing fall
As fell Thy manna down.

Drop Thy still dews of quietness,
Till all our strivings cease;
Take from our souls the strain and stress,
And let our ordered lives confess
The beauty of Thy peace.

Breathe through the heats of our desire
Thy coolness and Thy balm;
Let sense be dumb, let flesh retire;
Speak through the earthquake, wind, and fire,
O still, small voice of calm!
1872.

A WOMAN.

Oh, dwarfed and wronged, and stained with ill,
Behold! thou art a woman still!
And, by that sacred name and dear,
I bid thy better self appear.
Still, through thy foul disguise, I see
The rudimental purity,
That, spite of change and loss, makes good
Thy birthright—claim of womanhood;
An inward loathing, deep, intense;
A shame that is half innocence.
Cast off the grave—clothes of thy sin!
Rise from the dust thou liest in,
As Mary rose at Jesus' word,
Redeemed and white before the Lord!
Reclaim thy lost soul! In His name,

Rise up, and break thy bonds of shame.
Art weak? He 's strong. Art fearful? Hear
The world's O'ercomer: "Be of cheer!"
What lip shall judge when He approves?
Who dare to scorn the child He loves?

THE PRAYER OF AGASSIZ.

The island of Penikese in Buzzard's Bay was given by Mr. John
Anderson to Agassiz for the uses of a summer school of natural
history. A large barn was cleared and improvised as a lecture–room.
Here, on the first morning of the school, all the company was
gathered. "Agassiz had arranged no programme of exercises," says
Mrs. Agassiz, in Louis Agassiz; his Life and Correspondence,
"trusting to the interest of the occasion to suggest what might best
be said or done. But, as he looked upon his pupils gathered there
to study nature with him, by an impulse as natural as it was
unpremeditated, he called upon then to join in silently asking
God's blessing on their work together. The pause was broken by the
first words of an address no less fervent than its unspoken
prelude." This was in the summer of 1873, and Agassiz died the
December following.

On the isle of Penikese,
Ringed about by sapphire seas,
Fanned by breezes salt and cool,
Stood the Master with his school.
Over sails that not in vain
Wooed the west–wind's steady strain,
Line of coast that low and far
Stretched its undulating bar,
Wings aslant along the rim

Of the waves they stooped to skim,
Rock and isle and glistening bay,
Fell the beautiful white day.

Said the Master to the youth
"We have come in search of truth,
Trying with uncertain key
Door by door of mystery;
We are reaching, through His laws,
To the garment—hem of Cause,
Him, the endless, unbegun,
The Unnamable, the One
Light of all our light the Source,
Life of life, and Force of force.
As with fingers of the blind,
We are groping here to find
What the hieroglyphics mean
Of the Unseen in the seen,
What the Thought which underlies
Nature's masking and disguise,
What it is that hides beneath
Blight and bloom and birth and death.
By past efforts unavailing,
Doubt and error, loss and failing,
Of our weakness made aware,
On the threshold of our task
Let us light and guidance ask,
Let us pause in silent prayer!"

Then the Master in his place
Bowed his head a little space,
And the leaves by soft airs stirred,

345

Lapse of wave and cry of bird,
Left the solemn hush unbroken
Of that wordless prayer unspoken,
While its wish, on earth unsaid,
Rose to heaven interpreted.
As, in life's best hours, we hear
By the spirit's finer ear
His low voice within us, thus
The All–Father heareth us;
And His holy ear we pain
With our noisy words and vain.
Not for Him our violence
Storming at the gates of sense,
His the primal language, His
The eternal silences!

Even the careless heart was moved,
And the doubting gave assent,
With a gesture reverent,
To the Master well–beloved.
As thin mists are glorified
By the light they cannot hide,
All who gazed upon him saw,
Through its veil of tender awe,
How his face was still uplit
By the old sweet look of it.
Hopeful, trustful, full of cheer,
And the love that casts out fear.
Who the secret may declare
Of that brief, unuttered prayer?
Did the shade before him come
Of th' inevitable doom,
Of the end of earth so near,
And Eternity's new year?

In the lap of sheltering seas
Rests the isle of Penikese;
But the lord of the domain
Comes not to his own again
Where the eyes that follow fail,
On a vaster sea his sail
Drifts beyond our beck and hail.
Other lips within its bound
Shall the laws of life expound;
Other eyes from rock and shell
Read the world's old riddles well
But when breezes light and bland
Blow from Summer's blossomed land,
When the air is glad with wings,
And the blithe song–sparrow sings,
Many an eye with his still face
Shall the living ones displace,
Many an ear the word shall seek
He alone could fitly speak.
And one name forevermore
Shall be uttered o'er and o'er
By the waves that kiss the shore,
By the curlew's whistle sent
Down the cool, sea–scented air;
In all voices known to her,
Nature owns her worshipper,
Half in triumph, half lament.
Thither Love shall tearful turn,
Friendship pause uncovered there,
And the wisest reverence learn
From the Master's silent prayer.
1873.

IN QUEST

Have I not voyaged, friend beloved, with thee
On the great waters of the unsounded sea,
Momently listening with suspended oar
For the low rote of waves upon a shore
Changeless as heaven, where never fog–cloud drifts
Over its windless wood, nor mirage lifts
The steadfast hills; where never birds of doubt
Sing to mislead, and every dream dies out,
And the dark riddles which perplex us here
In the sharp solvent of its light are clear?
Thou knowest how vain our quest; how, soon or late,
The baffling tides and circles of debate
Swept back our bark unto its starting–place,
Where, looking forth upon the blank, gray space,
And round about us seeing, with sad eyes,
The same old difficult hills and cloud–cold skies,
We said: "This outward search availeth not
To find Him. He is farther than we thought,
Or, haply, nearer. To this very spot
Whereon we wait, this commonplace of home,
As to the well of Jacob, He may come
And tell us all things." As I listened there,
Through the expectant silences of prayer,
Somewhat I seemed to hear, which hath to me
Been hope, strength, comfort, and I give it thee.

"The riddle of the world is understood
Only by him who feels that God is good,
As only he can feel who makes his love

348

The ladder of his faith, and climbs above
On th' rounds of his best instincts; draws no line
Between mere human goodness and divine,
But, judging God by what in him is best,
With a child's trust leans on a Father's breast,
And hears unmoved the old creeds babble still
Of kingly power and dread caprice of will,
Chary of blessing, prodigal of curse,
The pitiless doomsman of the universe.
Can Hatred ask for love? Can Selfishness
Invite to self–denial? Is He less
Than man in kindly dealing? Can He break
His own great law of fatherhood, forsake
And curse His children? Not for earth and heaven
Can separate tables of the law be given.
No rule can bind which He himself denies;
The truths of time are not eternal lies."

So heard I; and the chaos round me spread
To light and order grew; and, "Lord," I said,
"Our sins are our tormentors, worst of all
Felt in distrustful shame that dares not call
Upon Thee as our Father. We have set
A strange god up, but Thou remainest yet.
All that I feel of pity Thou hast known
Before I was; my best is all Thy own.
From Thy great heart of goodness mine but drew
Wishes and prayers; but Thou, O Lord, wilt do,
In Thy own time, by ways I cannot see,
All that I feel when I am nearest Thee!"
1873.

THE FRIEND'S BURIAL.

My thoughts are all in yonder town,
Where, wept by many tears,
To—day my mother's friend lays down
The burden of her years.

True as in life, no poor disguise
Of death with her is seen,
And on her simple casket lies
No wreath of bloom and green.

Oh, not for her the florist's art,
The mocking weeds of woe;
Dear memories in each mourner's heart
Like heaven's white lilies blow.

And all about the softening air
Of new—born sweetness tells,
And the ungathered May—flowers wear
The tints of ocean shells.

The old, assuring miracle
Is fresh as heretofore;
And earth takes up its parable

Of life from death once more.

Here organ—swell and church—bell toll
Methinks but discord were;
The prayerful silence of the soul
Is best befitting her.

No sound should break the quietude
Alike of earth and sky
O wandering wind in Seabrook wood,
Breathe but a half—heard sigh!

Sing softly, spring—bird, for her sake;
And thou not distant sea,
Lapse lightly as if Jesus spake,
And thou wert Galilee!

For all her quiet life flowed on
As meadow streamlets flow,
Where fresher green reveals alone
The noiseless ways they go.

From her loved place of prayer I see
The plain—robed mourners pass,
With slow feet treading reverently
The graveyard's springing grass.

Make room, O mourning ones, for me,
Where, like the friends of Paul,
That you no more her face shall see
You sorrow most of all.

Her path shall brighten more and more
Unto the perfect day;
She cannot fail of peace who bore
Such peace with her away.

O sweet, calm face that seemed to wear
The look of sins forgiven!
O voice of prayer that seemed to bear
Our own needs up to heaven!

How reverent in our midst she stood,
Or knelt in grateful praise!
What grace of Christian womanhood
Was in her household ways!

For still her holy living meant
No duty left undone;
The heavenly and the human blent
Their kindred loves in one.

And if her life small leisure found
For feasting ear and eye,
And Pleasure, on her daily round,
She passed unpausing by,

Yet with her went a secret sense
Of all things sweet and fair,
And Beauty's gracious providence
Refreshed her unaware.

She kept her line of rectitude
With love's unconscious ease;
Her kindly instincts understood
All gentle courtesies.

An inborn charm of graciousness
Made sweet her smile and tone,
And glorified her farm–wife dress
With beauty not its own.

The dear Lord's best interpreters
Are humble human souls;
The Gospel of a life like hers
Is more than books or scrolls.

From scheme and creed the light goes out,
The saintly fact survives;
The blessed Master none can doubt
Revealed in holy lives.
1873.

A CHRISTMAS CARMEN.

I.
Sound over all waters, reach out from all lands,
The chorus of voices, the clasping of hands;
Sing hymns that were sung by the stars of the morn,
Sing songs of the angels when Jesus was born!
With glad jubilations
Bring hope to the nations
The dark night is ending and dawn has begun
Rise, hope of the ages, arise like the sun,
All speech flow to music, all hearts beat as one!

II.
Sing the bridal of nations! with chorals of love
Sing out the war–vulture and sing in the dove,
Till the hearts of the peoples keep time in accord,
And the voice of the world is the voice of the Lord!
Clasp hands of the nations
In strong gratulations:
The dark night is ending and dawn has begun;
Rise, hope of the ages, arise like the sun,
All speech flow to music, all hearts beat as one!

III.
Blow, bugles of battle, the marches of peace;
East, west, north, and south let the long quarrel cease
Sing the song of great joy that the angels began,
Sing of glory to God and of good—will to man!
Hark! joining in chorus
The heavens bend o'er us'
The dark night is ending and dawn has begun;
Rise, hope of the ages, arise like the sun,
All speech flow to music, all hearts beat as one!
1873.

VESTA.

O Christ of God! whose life and death
Our own have reconciled,
Most quietly, most tenderly
Take home Thy star—named child!

Thy grace is in her patient eyes,
Thy words are on her tongue;
The very silence round her seems
As if the angels sung.

Her smile is as a listening child's
Who hears its mother call;
The lilies of Thy perfect peace
About her pillow fall.

She leans from out our clinging arms
To rest herself in Thine;
Alone to Thee, dear Lord, can we
Our well–beloved resign!

Oh, less for her than for ourselves
We bow our heads and pray;
Her setting star, like Bethlehem's,
To Thee shall point the way!
1874.

CHILD–SONGS.

Still linger in our noon of time
And on our Saxon tongue
The echoes of the home–born hymns
The Aryan mothers sung.

And childhood had its litanies
In every age and clime;
The earliest cradles of the race
Were rocked to poet's rhyme.

Nor sky, nor wave, nor tree, nor flower,

Nor green earth's virgin sod,
So moved the singer's heart of old
As these small ones of God.

The mystery of unfolding life
Was more than dawning morn,
Than opening flower or crescent moon
The human soul new–born.

And still to childhood's sweet appeal
The heart of genius turns,
And more than all the sages teach
From lisping voices learns,—

The voices loved of him who sang,
Where Tweed and Teviot glide,
That sound to–day on all the winds
That blow from Rydal–side,—

Heard in the Teuton's household songs,
And folk–lore of the Finn,
Where'er to holy Christmas hearths
The Christ–child enters in!

Before life's sweetest mystery still
The heart in reverence kneels;

357

The wonder of the primal birth
The latest mother feels.

We need love's tender lessons taught
As only weakness can;
God hath His small interpreters;
The child must teach the man.

We wander wide through evil years,
Our eyes of faith grow dim;
But he is freshest from His hands
And nearest unto Him!

And haply, pleading long with Him
For sin—sick hearts and cold,
The angels of our childhood still
The Father's face behold.

Of such the kingdom!—Teach Thou us,
O—Master most divine,
To feel the deep significance
Of these wise words of Thine!

The haughty eye shall seek in vain
What innocence beholds;
No cunning finds the key of heaven,

358

No strength its gate unfolds.

Alone to guilelessness and love
That gate shall open fall;
The mind of pride is nothingness,
The childlike heart is all!
1875.

THE HEALER.

TO A YOUNG PHYSICIAN, WITH DORE'S PICTURE OF CHRIST
HEALING THE SICK.

So stood of old the holy Christ
Amidst the suffering throng;
With whom His lightest touch sufficed
To make the weakest strong.

That healing gift He lends to them
Who use it in His name;
The power that filled His garment's hem
Is evermore the same.

For lo! in human hearts unseen
The Healer dwelleth still,
And they who make His temples clean

The best subserve His will.

The holiest task by Heaven decreed,
An errand all divine,
The burden of our common need
To render less is thine.

The paths of pain are thine. Go forth
With patience, trust, and hope;
The sufferings of a sin–sick earth
Shall give thee ample scope.

Beside the unveiled mysteries
Of life and death go stand,
With guarded lips and reverent eyes
And pure of heart and hand.

So shalt thou be with power endued
From Him who went about
The Syrian hillsides doing good,
And casting demons out.

That Good Physician liveth yet
Thy friend and guide to be;
The Healer by Gennesaret
Shall walk the rounds with thee.

THE TWO ANGELS.

God called the nearest angels who dwell with Him above:
The tenderest one was Pity, the dearest one was Love.

"Arise," He said, "my angels! a wail of woe and sin
Steals through the gates of heaven, and saddens all within.

"My harps take up the mournful strain that from a lost world swells,
The smoke of torment clouds the light and blights the asphodels.

"Fly downward to that under world, and on its souls of pain
Let Love drop smiles like sunshine, and Pity tears like rain!"

Two faces bowed before the Throne, veiled in their golden hair;
Four white wings lessened swiftly down the dark abyss of air.

The way was strange, the flight was long; at last the angels came
Where swung the lost and nether world, red—wrapped in rayless flame.

There Pity, shuddering, wept; but Love, with faith too strong for fear,

Took heart from God's almightiness and smiled a smile of cheer.

And lo! that tear of Pity quenched the flame whereon it fell,
And, with the sunshine of that smile, hope entered into hell!

Two unveiled faces full of joy looked upward to the Throne,
Four white wings folded at the feet of Him who sat thereon!

And deeper than the sound of seas, more soft than falling flake,
Amidst the hush of wing and song the Voice Eternal spake:

"Welcome, my angels! ye have brought a holier joy to heaven;
Henceforth its sweetest song shall be the song of sin forgiven!"
1875.

OVERRULED.

The threads our hands in blindness spin
No self–determined plan weaves in;
The shuttle of the unseen powers
Works out a pattern not as ours.

Ah! small the choice of him who sings

What sound shall leave the smitten strings;
Fate holds and guides the hand of art;
The singer's is the servant's part.

The wind—harp chooses not the tone
That through its trembling threads is blown;
The patient organ cannot guess
What hand its passive keys shall press.

Through wish, resolve, and act, our will
Is moved by undreamed forces still;
And no man measures in advance
His strength with untried circumstance.

As streams take hue from shade and sun,
As runs the life the song must run;
But, glad or sad, to His good end
God grant the varying notes may tend!
1877.

HYMN OF THE DUNKERS

KLOSTER KEDAR, EPHRATA, PENNSYLVANIA (1738)

SISTER MARIA CHRISTINA sings

363

Wake, sisters, wake! the day—star shines;
Above Ephrata's eastern pines
The dawn is breaking, cool and calm.
Wake, sisters, wake to prayer and psalm!

Praised be the Lord for shade and light,
For toil by day, for rest by night!
Praised be His name who deigns to bless
Our Kedar of the wilderness!

Our refuge when the spoiler's hand
Was heavy on our native land;
And freedom, to her children due,
The wolf and vulture only knew.

We praised Him when to prison led,
We owned Him when the stake blazed red;
We knew, whatever might befall,
His love and power were over all.

He heard our prayers; with outstretched arm
He led us forth from cruel harm;
Still, wheresoe'er our steps were bent,
His cloud and fire before us went!

The watch of faith and prayer He set,
We kept it then, we keep it yet.
At midnight, crow of cock, or noon,
He cometh sure, He cometh soon.

He comes to chasten, not destroy,
To purge the earth from sin's alloy.
At last, at last shall all confess
His mercy as His righteousness.

The dead shall live, the sick be whole,
The scarlet sin be white as wool;
No discord mar below, above,
The music of eternal love!

Sound, welcome trump, the last alarm!
Lord God of hosts, make bare thine arm,
Fulfil this day our long desire,
Make sweet and clean the world with fire!

Sweep, flaming besom, sweep from sight
The lies of time; be swift to smite,
Sharp sword of God, all idols down,
Genevan creed and Roman crown.

Quake, earth, through all thy zones, till all
The fanes of pride and priesteraft fall;
And lift thou up in place of them
Thy gates of pearl, Jerusalem!

Lo! rising from baptismal flame,
Transfigured, glorious, yet the same,
Within the heavenly city's bound
Our Kloster Kedar shall be found.

He cometh soon! at dawn or noon
Or set of sun, He cometh soon.
Our prayers shall meet Him on His way;
Wake, sisters, wake! arise and pray!
1877.

GIVING AND TAKING.

I have attempted to put in English verse a prose translation of a
poem by Tinnevaluva, a Hindoo poet of the third century of our era.

Who gives and hides the giving hand,
Nor counts on favor, fame, or praise,
Shall find his smallest gift outweighs
The burden of the sea and land.

Who gives to whom hath naught been given,
His gift in need, though small indeed
As is the grass–blade's wind–blown seed,
Is large as earth and rich as heaven.

Forget it not, O man, to whom
A gift shall fall, while yet on earth;
Yea, even to thy seven–fold birth
Recall it in the lives to come.

Who broods above a wrong in thought
Sins much; but greater sin is his
Who, fed and clothed with kindnesses,
Shall count the holy alms as nought.

Who dares to curse the hands that bless
Shall know of sin the deadliest cost;
The patience of the heavens is lost
Beholding man's unthankfulness.

For he who breaks all laws may still
In Sivam's mercy be forgiven;
But none can save, in earth or heaven,
The wretch who answers good with ill.
1877.

THE VISION OF ECHARD.

The Benedictine Echard
Sat by the wayside well,
Where Marsberg sees the bridal
Of the Sarre and the Moselle.

Fair with its sloping vineyards
And tawny chestnut bloom,
The happy vale Ausonius sunk
For holy Treves made room.

On the shrine Helena builded
To keep the Christ coat well,
On minster tower and kloster cross,
The westering sunshine fell.

There, where the rock–hewn circles
O'erlooked the Roman's game,
The veil of sleep fell on him,
And his thought a dream became.

He felt the heart of silence
Throb with a soundless word,
And by the inward ear alone

A spirit's voice he heard.

And the spoken word seemed written
On air and wave and sod,
And the bending walls of sapphire
Blazed with the thought of God.

"What lack I, O my children?
All things are in my band;
The vast earth and the awful stars
I hold as grains of sand.

"Need I your alms? The silver
And gold are mine alone;
The gifts ye bring before me
Were evermore my own.

"Heed I the noise of viols,
Your pomp of masque and show?
Have I not dawns and sunsets
Have I not winds that blow?

"Do I smell your gums of incense?
Is my ear with chantings fed?
Taste I your wine of worship,
Or eat your holy bread?

"Of rank and name and honors
Am I vain as ye are vain?
What can Eternal Fulness
From your lip–service gain?

"Ye make me not your debtor
Who serve yourselves alone;
Ye boast to me of homage
Whose gain is all your own.

"For you I gave the prophets,
For you the Psalmist's lay
For you the law's stone tables,
And holy book and day.

"Ye change to weary burdens
The helps that should uplift;
Ye lose in form the spirit,
The Giver in the gift.

"Who called ye to self–torment,
To fast and penance vain?
Dream ye Eternal Goodness
Has joy in mortal pain?

"For the death in life of Nitria,
For your Chartreuse ever dumb,
What better is the neighbor,
Or happier the home?

"Who counts his brother's welfare
As sacred as his own,
And loves, forgives, and pities,
He serveth me alone.

"I note each gracious purpose,
Each kindly word and deed;
Are ye not all my children?
Shall not the Father heed?

"No prayer for light and guidance
Is lost upon mine ear
The child's cry in the darkness
Shall not the Father hear?

"I loathe your wrangling councils,
I tread upon your creeds;
Who made ye mine avengers,
Or told ye of my needs;

"I bless men and ye curse them,
I love them and ye hate;
Ye bite and tear each other,
I suffer long and wait.

"Ye bow to ghastly symbols,
To cross and scourge and thorn;
Ye seek his Syrian manger
Who in the heart is born.

"For the dead Christ, not the living,
Ye watch His empty grave,
Whose life alone within you
Has power to bless and save.

"O blind ones, outward groping,
The idle quest forego;
Who listens to His inward voice
Alone of Him shall know.

"His love all love exceeding
The heart must needs recall,
Its self—surrendering freedom,
Its loss that gaineth all.

372

"Climb not the holy mountains,
Their eagles know not me;
Seek not the Blessed Islands,
I dwell not in the sea.

"Gone is the mount of Meru,
The triple gods are gone,
And, deaf to all the lama's prayers,
The Buddha slumbers on.

"No more from rocky Horeb
The smitten waters gush;
Fallen is Bethel's ladder,
Quenched is the burning bush.

"The jewels of the Urim
And Thurnmim all are dim;
The fire has left the altar,
The sign the teraphim.

"No more in ark or hill grove
The Holiest abides;
Not in the scroll's dead letter
The eternal secret hides.

"The eye shall fail that searches
For me the hollow sky;
The far is even as the near,
The low is as the high.

"What if the earth is hiding
Her old faiths, long outworn?
What is it to the changeless truth
That yours shall fail in turn?

"What if the o'erturned altar
Lays bare the ancient lie?
What if the dreams and legends
Of the world's childhood die?

"Have ye not still my witness
Within yourselves alway,
My hand that on the keys of life
For bliss or bale I lay?

"Still, in perpetual judgment,
I hold assize within,
With sure reward of holiness,
And dread rebuke of sin.

"A light, a guide, a warning,
A presence ever near,
Through the deep silence of the flesh
I reach the inward ear.

"My Gerizim and Ebal
Are in each human soul,
The still, small voice of blessing,
And Sinai's thunder—roll.

"The stern behest of duty,
The doom—book open thrown,
The heaven ye seek, the hell ye fear,
Are with yourselves alone."

. . . . .

A gold and purple sunset
Flowed down the broad Moselle;
On hills of vine and meadow lands
The peace of twilight fell.

A slow, cool wind of evening
Blew over leaf and bloom;
And, faint and far, the Angelus
Rang from Saint Matthew's tomb.

Then up rose Master Echard,
And marvelled: "Can it be
That here, in dream and vision,
The Lord hath talked with me?"

He went his way; behind him
The shrines of saintly dead,
The holy coat and nail of cross,
He left unvisited.

He sought the vale of Eltzbach
His burdened soul to free,
Where the foot–hills of the Eifel
Are glassed in Laachersee.

And, in his Order's kloster,
He sat, in night–long parle,
With Tauler of the Friends of God,
And Nicolas of Basle.

And lo! the twain made answer
"Yea, brother, even thus
The Voice above all voices
Hath spoken unto us.

"The world will have its idols,
And flesh and sense their sign
But the blinded eyes shall open,
And the gross ear be fine.

"What if the vision tarry?
God's time is always best;
The true Light shall be witnessed,
The Christ within confessed.

"In mercy or in judgment
He shall turn and overturn,
Till the heart shall be His temple
Where all of Him shall learn."

INSCRIPTIONS.

ON A SUN–DIAL.

FOR DR. HENRY I. BOWDITCH.

With warning hand I mark Time's rapid flight
From life's glad morning to its solemn night;
Yet, through the dear God's love, I also show

377

There's Light above me by the Shade below.
1879.

ON A FOUNTAIN.

FOR DOROTHEA L. DIX.

Stranger and traveller,
Drink freely and bestow
A kindly thought on her
Who bade this fountain flow,
Yet hath no other claim
Than as the minister
Of blessing in God's name.
Drink, and in His peace go
1879

THE MINISTER'S DAUGHTER.

In the minister's morning sermon
He had told of the primal fall,
And how thenceforth the wrath of God
Rested on each and all.

And how of His will and pleasure,
All souls, save a chosen few,
Were doomed to the quenchless burning,
And held in the way thereto.

Yet never by faith's unreason
A saintlier soul was tried,
And never the harsh old lesson
A tenderer heart belied.

And, after the painful service
On that pleasant Sabbath day,
He walked with his little daughter
Through the apple–bloom of May.

Sweet in the fresh green meadows
Sparrow and blackbird sung;
Above him their tinted petals
The blossoming orchards hung.

Around on the wonderful glory
The minister looked and smiled;
"How good is the Lord who gives us
These gifts from His hand, my child.

"Behold in the bloom of apples
And the violets in the sward
A hint of the old, lost beauty
Of the Garden of the Lord!"

Then up spake the little maiden,
Treading on snow and pink
"O father! these pretty blossoms
Are very wicked, I think.

"Had there been no Garden of Eden
There never had been a fall;
And if never a tree had blossomed
God would have loved us all."

"Hush, child!" the father answered,
"By His decree man fell;
His ways are in clouds and darkness,
But He doeth all things well.

"And whether by His ordaining
To us cometh good or ill,
Joy or pain, or light or shadow,
We must fear and love Him still."

"Oh, I fear Him!" said the daughter,
"And I try to love Him, too;
But I wish He was good and gentle,
Kind and loving as you."

The minister groaned in spirit
As the tremulous lips of pain
And wide, wet eyes uplifted
Questioned his own in vain.

Bowing his head he pondered
The words of the little one;
Had he erred in his life–long teaching?
Had he wrong to his Master done?

To what grim and dreadful idol
Had he lent the holiest name?
Did his own heart, loving and human,
The God of his worship shame?

And lo! from the bloom and greenness,
From the tender skies above,
And the face of his little daughter,
He read a lesson of love.

No more as the cloudy terror
Of Sinai's mount of law,
But as Christ in the Syrian lilies
The vision of God he saw.

And, as when, in the clefts of Horeb,
Of old was His presence known,
The dread Ineffable Glory
Was Infinite Goodness alone.

Thereafter his hearers noted
In his prayers a tenderer strain,
And never the gospel of hatred
Burned on his lips again.

And the scoffing tongue was prayerful,
And the blinded eyes found sight,
And hearts, as flint aforetime,
Grew soft in his warmth and light.
1880.

BY THEIR WORKS.

Call him not heretic whose works attest
His faith in goodness by no creed confessed.
Whatever in love's name is truly done

To free the bound and lift the fallen one
Is done to Christ. Whoso in deed and word
Is not against Him labors for our Lord.
When He, who, sad and weary, longing sore
For love's sweet service, sought the sisters' door,
One saw the heavenly, one the human guest,
But who shall say which loved the Master best?
1881.

THE WORD.

Voice of the Holy Spirit, making known
Man to himself, a witness swift and sure,
Warning, approving, true and wise and pure,
Counsel and guidance that misleadeth none!
By thee the mystery of life is read;
The picture—writing of the world's gray seers,
The myths and parables of the primal years,
Whose letter kills, by thee interpreted
Take healthful meanings fitted to our needs,
And in the soul's vernacular express
The common law of simple righteousness.
Hatred of cant and doubt of human creeds
May well be felt: the unpardonable sin
Is to deny the Word of God within!
1881.

THE BOOK.

Gallery of sacred pictures manifold,
A minster rich in holy effigies,

And bearing on entablature and frieze
The hieroglyphic oracles of old.
Along its transept aureoled martyrs sit;
And the low chancel side–lights half acquaint
The eye with shrines of prophet, bard, and saint,
Their age–dimmed tablets traced in doubtful writ!
But only when on form and word obscure
Falls from above the white supernal light
We read the mystic characters aright,
And life informs the silent portraiture,
Until we pause at last, awe–held, before
The One ineffable Face, love, wonder, and adore.
1881

REQUIREMENT.

We live by Faith; but Faith is not the slave
Of text and legend. Reason's voice and God's,
Nature's and Duty's, never are at odds.
What asks our Father of His children, save
Justice and mercy and humility,
A reasonable service of good deeds,
Pure living, tenderness to human needs,
Reverence and trust, and prayer for light to see
The Master's footprints in our daily ways?
No knotted scourge nor sacrificial knife,
But the calm beauty of an ordered life
Whose very breathing is unworded praise!—
A life that stands as all true lives have stood,
Firm–rooted in the faith that God is Good.
1881.

HELP.

Dream not, O Soul, that easy is the task
Thus set before thee. If it proves at length,
As well it may, beyond thy natural strength,
Faint not, despair not. As a child may ask
A father, pray the Everlasting Good
For light and guidance midst the subtle snares
Of sin thick planted in life's thoroughfares,
For spiritual strength and moral hardihood;
Still listening, through the noise of time and sense,
To the still whisper of the Inward Word;
Bitter in blame, sweet in approval heard,
Itself its own confirming evidence
To health of soul a voice to cheer and please,
To guilt the wrath of the Eumenides.
1881.

UTTERANCE.

But what avail inadequate words to reach
The innermost of Truth? Who shall essay,
Blinded and weak, to point and lead the way,
Or solve the mystery in familiar speech?
Yet, if it be that something not thy own,
Some shadow of the Thought to which our schemes,
Creeds, cult, and ritual are at best but dreams,
Is even to thy unworthiness made known,
Thou mayst not hide what yet thou shouldst not dare
To utter lightly, lest on lips of thine
The real seem false, the beauty undivine.

**So, weighing duty in the scale of prayer,
Give what seems given thee. It may prove a seed
Of goodness dropped in fallow–grounds of need.
1881.**

ORIENTAL MAXIMS.

PARAPHRASE OF SANSCRIT TRANSLATIONS.

THE INWARD JUDGE.

From Institutes of Manu.

The soul itself its awful witness is.
Say not in evil doing, "No one sees,"
And so offend the conscious One within,
Whose ear can hear the silences of sin.

Ere they find voice, whose eyes unsleeping see
The secret motions of iniquity.
Nor in thy folly say, "I am alone."
For, seated in thy heart, as on a throne,
The ancient Judge and Witness liveth still,
To note thy act and thought; and as thy ill

Or good goes from thee, far beyond thy reach,
The solemn Doomsman's seal is set on each.
1878.

LAYING UP TREASURE

From the Mahabharata.

Before the Ender comes, whose charioteer
Is swift or slow Disease, lay up each year
Thy harvests of well–doing, wealth that kings
Nor thieves can take away. When all the things
Thou tallest thine, goods, pleasures, honors fall,
Thou in thy virtue shalt survive them all.
1881.

CONDUCT

From the Mahabharata.

Heed how thou livest. Do no act by day
Which from the night shall drive thy peace away.
In months of sun so live that months of rain
Shall still be happy. Evermore restrain
Evil and cherish good, so shall there be
Another and a happier life for thee.
1881.

AN EASTER FLOWER GIFT.

O dearest bloom the seasons know,
Flowers of the Resurrection blow,
Our hope and faith restore;
And through the bitterness of death
And loss and sorrow, breathe a breath
Of life forevermore!

The thought of Love Immortal blends
With fond remembrances of friends;
In you, O sacred flowers,
By human love made doubly sweet,
The heavenly and the earthly meet,
The heart of Christ and ours!
1882.

THE MYSTIC'S CHRISTMAS.

"All hail!" the bells of Christmas rang,
"All hail!" the monks at Christmas sang,
The merry monks who kept with cheer
The gladdest day of all their year.

But still apart, unmoved thereat,
A pious elder brother sat
Silent, in his accustomed place,

With God's sweet peace upon his face.

"Why sitt'st thou thus?" his brethren cried.
"It is the blessed Christmas—tide;
The Christmas lights are all aglow,
The sacred lilies bud and blow.

"Above our heads the joy—bells ring,
Without the happy children sing,
And all God's creatures hail the morn
On which the holy Christ was born!

"Rejoice with us; no more rebuke
Our gladness with thy quiet look."
The gray monk answered: "Keep, I pray,
Even as ye list, the Lord's birthday.

"Let heathen Yule fires flicker red
Where thronged refectory feasts are spread;
With mystery—play and masque and mime
And wait—songs speed the holy time!

"The blindest faith may haply save;
The Lord accepts the things we have;
And reverence, howsoe'er it strays,
May find at last the shining ways.

389

"They needs must grope who cannot see,
The blade before the ear must be;
As ye are feeling I have felt,
And where ye dwell I too have dwelt.

"But now, beyond the things of sense,
Beyond occasions and events,
I know, through God's exceeding grace,
Release from form and time and place.

"I listen, from no mortal tongue,
To hear the song the angels sung;
And wait within myself to know
The Christmas lilies bud and blow.

"The outward symbols disappear
From him whose inward sight is clear;
And small must be the choice of clays
To him who fills them all with praise!

"Keep while you need it, brothers mine,
With honest zeal your Christmas sign,
But judge not him who every morn
Feels in his heart the Lord Christ born!"
1882.

AT LAST.

When on my day of life the night is falling,
And, in the winds from unsunned spaces blown,
I hear far voices out of darkness calling
My feet to paths unknown,

Thou who hast made my home of life so pleasant,
Leave not its tenant when its walls decay;
O Love Divine, O Helper ever present,
Be Thou my strength and stay!

Be near me when all else is from me drifting
Earth, sky, home's pictures, days of shade and shine,
And kindly faces to my own uplifting
The love which answers mine.

I have but Thee, my Father! let Thy spirit
Be with me then to comfort and uphold;
No gate of pearl, no branch of palm I merit,
Nor street of shining gold.

Suffice it if—my good and ill unreckoned,
And both forgiven through Thy abounding grace—
I find myself by hands familiar beckoned

Unto my fitting place.

Some humble door among Thy many mansions,
Some sheltering shade where sin and striving cease,
And flows forever through heaven's green expansions
The river of Thy peace.

There, from the music round about me stealing,
I fain would learn the new and holy song,
And find at last, beneath Thy trees of healing,
The life for which I long.
1882

WHAT THE TRAVELLER SAID AT SUNSET.

The shadows grow and deepen round me,
I feel the deffall in the air;
The muezzin of the darkening thicket,
I hear the night–thrush call to prayer.

The evening wind is sad with farewells,
And loving hands unclasp from mine;
Alone I go to meet the darkness
Across an awful boundary–line.

As from the lighted hearths behind me
I pass with slow, reluctant feet,
What waits me in the land of strangeness?
What face shall smile, what voice shall greet?

What space shall awe, what brightness blind me?
What thunder—roll of music stun?
What vast processions sweep before me
Of shapes unknown beneath the sun?

I shrink from unaccustomed glory,
I dread the myriad—voiced strain;
Give me the unforgotten faces,
And let my lost ones speak again.

He will not chide my mortal yearning
Who is our Brother and our Friend;
In whose full life, divine and human,
The heavenly and the earthly blend.

Mine be the joy of soul—communion,
The sense of spiritual strength renewed,
The reverence for the pure and holy,
The dear delight of doing good.

No fitting ear is mine to listen
An endless anthem's rise and fall;
No curious eye is mine to measure
The pearl gate and the jasper wall.

For love must needs be more than knowledge:
What matter if I never know
Why Aldebaran's star is ruddy,
Or warmer Sirius white as snow!

Forgive my human words, O Father!
I go Thy larger truth to prove;
Thy mercy shall transcend my longing
I seek but love, and Thou art Love!

I go to find my lost and mourned for
Safe in Thy sheltering goodness still,
And all that hope and faith foreshadow
Made perfect in Thy holy will!
1883.

THE "STORY OF IDA."

Francesca Alexander, whose pen and pencil have so reverently
transcribed the simple faith and life of the Italian peasantry,
wrote the narrative published with John Ruskin's introduction under
the title, *The Story of Ida*.

Weary of jangling noises never stilled,
The skeptic's sneer, the bigot's hate, the din
Of clashing texts, the webs of creed men spin
Round simple truth, the children grown who build
With gilded cards their new Jerusalem,
Busy, with sacerdotal tailorings
And tinsel gauds, bedizening holy things,
I turn, with glad and grateful heart, from them
To the sweet story of the Florentine
Immortal in her blameless maidenhood,
Beautiful as God's angels and as good;
Feeling that life, even now, may be divine
With love no wrong can ever change to hate,
No sin make less than all–compassionate!
1884.

THE LIGHT THAT IS FELT.

A tender child of summers three,
Seeking her little bed at night,
Paused on the dark stair timidly.
"Oh, mother! Take my hand," said she,
"And then the dark will all be light."

We older children grope our way
From dark behind to dark before;
And only when our hands we lay,
Dear Lord, in Thine, the night is day,

And there is darkness nevermore.

Reach downward to the sunless days
Wherein our guides are blind as we,
And faith is small and hope delays;
Take Thou the hands of prayer we raise,
And let us feel the light of Thee!
1884.

THE TWO LOVES

Smoothing soft the nestling head
Of a maiden fancy–led,
Thus a grave–eyed woman said:

"Richest gifts are those we make,
Dearer than the love we take
That we give for love's own sake.

"Well I know the heart's unrest;
Mine has been the common quest,
To be loved and therefore blest.

"Favors undeserved were mine;
At my feet as on a shrine

Love has laid its gifts divine.

"Sweet the offerings seemed, and yet
With their sweetness came regret,
And a sense of unpaid debt.

"Heart of mine unsatisfied,
Was it vanity or pride
That a deeper joy denied?

"Hands that ope but to receive
Empty close; they only live
Richly who can richly give.

"Still," she sighed, with moistening eyes,
"Love is sweet in any guise;
But its best is sacrifice!

"He who, giving, does not crave
Likest is to Him who gave
Life itself the loved to save.

"Love, that self–forgetful gives,
Sows surprise of ripened sheaves,

Late or soon its own receives."
1884.

ADJUSTMENT.

The tree of Faith its bare, dry boughs must shed
That nearer heaven the living ones may climb;
The false must fail, though from our shores of time
The old lament be heard, "Great Pan is dead!"
That wail is Error's, from his high place hurled;
This sharp recoil is Evil undertrod;
Our time's unrest, an angel sent of God
Troubling with life the waters of the world.
Even as they list the winds of the Spirit blow
To turn or break our century–rusted vanes;
Sands shift and waste; the rock alone remains
Where, led of Heaven, the strong tides come and go,
And storm–clouds, rent by thunderbolt and wind,
Leave, free of mist, the permanent stars behind.

Therefore I trust, although to outward sense
Both true and false seem shaken; I will hold
With newer light my reverence for the old,
And calmly wait the births of Providence.
No gain is lost; the clear–eyed saints look down
Untroubled on the wreck of schemes and creeds;
Love yet remains, its rosary of good deeds
Counting in task–field and o'erpeopled town;
Truth has charmed life; the Inward Word survives,
And, day by day, its revelation brings;
Faith, hope, and charity, whatsoever things

Which cannot be shaken, stand. Still holy lives
Reveal the Christ of whom the letter told,
And the new gospel verifies the old.
1885.

HYMNS OF THE BRAHMO SOMAJ.

I have attempted this paraphrase of the Hymns of the Brahmo Somaj
of India, as I find them in Mozoomdar's account of the devotional
exercises of that remarkable religious development which has
attracted far less attention and sympathy from the Christian world
than it deserves, as a fresh revelation of the direct action of the
Divine Spirit upon the human heart.

I.
The mercy, O Eternal One!
By man unmeasured yet,
In joy or grief, in shade or sun,
I never will forget.
I give the whole, and not a part,
Of all Thou gayest me;
My goods, my life, my soul and heart,
I yield them all to Thee!

II.
We fast and plead, we weep and pray,
From morning until even;
We feel to find the holy way,
We knock at the gate of heaven
And when in silent awe we wait,

And word and sign forbear,
The hinges of the golden gate
Move, soundless, to our prayer!
Who hears the eternal harmonies
Can heed no outward word;
Blind to all else is he who sees
The vision of the Lord!

III.
O soul, be patient, restrain thy tears,
Have hope, and not despair;
As a tender mother heareth her child
God hears the penitent prayer.
And not forever shall grief be thine;
On the Heavenly Mother's breast,
Washed clean and white in the waters of joy
Shall His seeking child find rest.
Console thyself with His word of grace,
And cease thy wail of woe,
For His mercy never an equal hath,
And His love no bounds can know.
Lean close unto Him in faith and hope;
How many like thee have found
In Him a shelter and home of peace,
By His mercy compassed round!
There, safe from sin and the sorrow it brings,
They sing their grateful psalms,
And rest, at noon, by the wells of God,
In the shade of His holy palms!
1885.

REVELATION.

"And I went into the Vale of Beavor, and as I went I preached
repentance to the people. And one morning, sitting by the fire, a
great cloud came over me, and a temptation beset me. And it was
said: All things come by Nature; and the Elements and the Stars
came over me. And as I sat still and let it alone, a living hope
arose in me, and a true Voice which said: There is a living God who
made all things. And immediately the cloud and the temptation
vanished, and Life rose over all, and my heart was glad and I
praised the Living God."—Journal of George Fox,
1690.

Still, as of old, in Beavor's Vale,
O man of God! our hope and faith
The Elements and Stars assail,
And the awed spirit holds its breath,
Blown over by a wind of death.

Takes Nature thought for such as we,
What place her human atom fills,
The weed–drift of her careless sea,
The mist on her unheeding hills?
What reeks she of our helpless wills?

Strange god of Force, with fear, not love,
Its trembling worshipper! Can prayer
Reach the shut ear of Fate, or move

Unpitying Energy to spare?
What doth the cosmic Vastness care?

In vain to this dread Unconcern
For the All–Father's love we look;
In vain, in quest of it, we turn
The storied leaves of Nature's book,
The prints her rocky tablets took.

I pray for faith, I long to trust;
I listen with my heart, and hear
A Voice without a sound: "Be just,
Be true, be merciful, revere
The Word within thee: God is near!

"A light to sky and earth unknown
Pales all their lights: a mightier force
Than theirs the powers of Nature own,
And, to its goal as at its source,
His Spirit moves the Universe.

"Believe and trust. Through stars and suns,
Through life and death, through soul and sense,
His wise, paternal purpose runs;
The darkness of His providence
Is star–lit with benign intents."

O joy supreme! I know the Voice,
Like none beside on earth or sea;
Yea, more, O soul of mine, rejoice,
By all that He requires of me,
I know what God himself must be.

No picture to my aid I call,
I shape no image in my prayer;
I only know in Him is all
Of life, light, beauty, everywhere,
Eternal Goodness here and there!

I know He is, and what He is,
Whose one great purpose is the good
Of all. I rest my soul on His
Immortal Love and Fatherhood;
And trust Him, as His children should.

I fear no more. The clouded face
Of Nature smiles; through all her things
Of time and space and sense I trace
The moving of the Spirit's wings,
And hear the song of hope she sings.
1886

Printed in the United States
148761LV00003B/14/A